"IT PROBABLY MEANT SOMETHING TO DO WITH BEING VERY ANTI-CHRISTIAN...IT WAS REALLY ABOUT SORT OF REDISCOVERING ALL THE **TABOOS** THAT HAVE BEEN SWEPT UNDER THE CARPET. YOU KNOW ROCK & ROLL ULTIMATELY WAS SOMETHING THAT WAS PROBABLY BORN LONG BEFORE **JESUS CHRIST** WAS EVER ON THIS PLANET AND PROBABLY CAN GO WAY BACK INTO THOSE DAYS WHEN WE WERE ALL EXOTICALLY MESSING ABOUT IN THOSE OLD FAMOUS PAGAN LOVE RITUALS."

MALCOLM McLAREN

"YOU MUST HAVE THE <u>DEVIL</u> <u>IN</u> <u>YOU</u> TO SUCCEED IN ANY OF THE ARTS."

VOLTAIRE

"MAN, I HAVE THE <u>DEVIL</u> <u>IN</u> <u>ME</u>"

JERRY LEE LEWIS

THE HEARTBEAT OF THE DRAGON

The Occult Roots of Rock & Roll

THE HEARTBEAT OF THE DRAGON

The Occult Roots of Rock & Roll

MARK SPAULDING

Light Warrior Press, Ltd.
Sterling Heights, Michigan 48311

THE HEARTBEAT OF THE DRAGON

The Occult Roots of Rock & Roll

First Printing 1992

ISBN # 0-935897-50-X

Graphics, Cover Art, Layout, and Design by:
Gary and Sally Pike
Victory Productions
4735 Murray Road
Mayville, MI 48744
(517)-843-5324

Photo Credits

ACKNOWLEDGEMENTS

I would like to acknowledge those responsible for the production of this book: first, my loyal, faithful, and loving wife Kathy, whose expertise in composition and tolerant insight has turned this work into a tool of promise; my brother in Christ, partner, eternal friend, and fellow researcher Ray, whose help, support, and hours of dedicated service has been a Godsend in every sense of the word; my brother John and his son Scott whose part in the production of this book could not be overstated; my brother and sister Gary and Sally who have given selflessly in the production of this work with their time and artistic talents (The LORD bless you abundantly in all you do.); my sister Debbie whose help has not gone unnoticed by God; my brother and fearless warrior in Christ, Michael who spent a long night with a lost Rock & Roll drummer so that this Rock & Roller could spend an eternity in peace; as well as all those who believed in this vision (Suresh, Redge and Jan, Wayne, and many others), undergirding it with their love and prayers. Only in eternity will we find out just what your prayers accomplished in the production of this book. But most of all I want to give my loving homage to my Creator and Lord, Jesus Christ who gave His own life for me so that I might live FOREVER with Him. All Hail KING JESUS! Words cannot express my eternal gratitude to you. I love you.

CONTENTS

FORWARD

There is no possible way in one small book we will be able to share with you all of our incredible discoveries concerning the unusual topic of the connection between Rock & Roll and the occult. We have spent many years researching this connection and the results have been, to say the least, rather startling.

We are presently in the process of compiling more information on this subject which will eventually become a larger and more detailed volume. Because of the nature of the information that we have already uncovered, we felt the necessity to write the book that you are about to read.

Though many good books are already available on this subject, we think this one has a little different twist.

Why has this book been written? To expose darkness (Acts 26:18) and expose people to the LIGHT! (John 8:12)

> MARK SPAULDING & THE CHRISTIAN MILITIA
> THE WARRIORS OF LIGHT

INTRODUCTION

ROCK & ROLL: Two words that conjure up in the mind sounds of uncontrolled syncopation and images of pulsating human bodies gyrating in a state of total abandon; an almost involuntary physical response to some primal emotional drive surfacing from somewhere deep within the soul. Rock & Roll is more than just music...*much* more. It is a mindset for many, and for those who have bought into its philosophy, a total way of life. It is a power as tasty as the once forbidden fruit: a bite of which still yields the *same* reward.

I would have to term Rock & Roll a spiritual force rather than a style of music; a force to be worshiped by the unwitting followers who kneel at its altar, ensnared by its false lure of freedom of expression and individuality. Ahhhh...I hear you say, 'WORSHIPED? Isn't that a rather strong word?' Yes it is, but not one that I use lightly; for those trapped within its web know full well what I mean.

Whether it's Roger Daltrey singing, "Long live rock"; Ozzy Osbourne singing, "rock and roll is my religion and my law"; Joan Jett singing, "I love rock & roll"; or one of its still tightly ensnared contemporary originators, Chuck Berry singing, "Hail, hail, rock & roll"; no doubt they would agree, if they were honest, that though Rock & Roll has blessed them all with fame, fortune, and power, it has extracted more from their lives than it has ever given back. There is the pulse and the flow, the rhythm and the spirit. It can only be recognized and identified by the truly free. In essence, Rock & Roll is *not* music. It is the *HEARTBEAT OF THE DRAGON*.

CHAPTER 1

AND THEY WORSHIPED THE DRAGON

"...and the dragon gave him his power and seat, and great authority...And they worshipped the dragon which gave power unto the beast: and they worshipped the beast..."

Rev. 13:2,4

Dragons and beasts with power and authority...Right about now you might just be asking yourself, 'What does all this mean?' Well, allow me, if you will, to clarify.

Just who or what is this biblical character known as the *DRAGON* mentioned in the above scripture? He once was, and to this day remains, the rebel leader of a vast host of angelic beings who, as a result of their failed coup attempt against God, were cast out of Heaven way back at the dawning of time. This incident is recalled as the LORD spoke through the prophet Ezekiel in chapter 28 of the book of the Bible which bears his name. Ezekiel 28:14-16 states concerning this fallen angel:

"Thou art the annointed cherub that covereth; and I have set thee so: thou wast upon the holy mountain of God; thou hast walked up and down in the midst of the stones of fire.

Thou wast perfect in thy ways from the day that thou wast created, till iniquity was found in thee.

By the multitude of thy merchandise they have filled the midst of thee with violence, and thou hast sinned: therefore I will **cast thee as profane out of the mountain of God:** *and I will destroy thee, O covering cherub, from the midst of the stones of fire."*

Yes, this angelic anarchist and his angels were expelled from Heaven. Their temporary jurisdiction at this present time extends from earth to the distant realms of outer space.

In the very near future, however, this domain will be curtailed to the earth and the immediate atmosphere surrounding it. Though this notorious and homicidal archangel now enjoys a vast range of influence, as a result of a crushing defeat delivered during a future, major, angelic altercation with the holy angels of God led by the archangel Michael, the realm of space he now partially controls will become permanently off limits. If you look in the Bible once again, the report of this future banishment and defeat is also clearly stated. Revelation chapter 12 verses 7-9 explain:

> *"And there was war in heaven: Michael and his angels fought against the dragon: and the dragon fought and his angels and they prevailed not: neither was their place found anymore in heaven.* **And the great DRAGON was cast out,** *that old* **SERPENT** *called the* **DEVIL** *and* **SATAN**, *which deceiveth the whole world:* **he was cast out and his angels were cast out with him.** *"*

It is clear by the previous scriptures that not only is this infamous spirit creature known by the name "the dragon", but he has a multiplicity of other names by which he can be identified as well. These appellations, revealed in this scripture passage, such as the DEVIL, SATAN, and the SERPENT are also identities by which this same being is presently known. However, in the Book of Isaiah, the Bible calls him by still another name. In this additional scripture, it not only gives us this other name, it reveals its literal meaning. The Book of Isaiah, chapter 14, verse 12, contains this statement once again pertaining to the same biblical figure. It declares:

> *"How art thou fallen from heaven, O* **Lucifer** *son of the morning!"*

The Old Testament of the Bible was originally written in the Hebrew language. The Hebrew word in this scripture that is translated Lucifer is the word HEY-LEL (pron. hay-lale'), which means "the morning star". The word "lucifer" is also translated "light-bearing". So we have basically interpreted the meaning of the name Lucifer as: morning star/light-bearer or, as the Bible also says, "*son of the morning*". Lucifer was the first being created by God and before his rebellion was appointed as a special messenger to His throne. Many biblical exegetes also believe he led the angelic choirs of Heaven. That was his original position.

As we already mentioned, Lucifer is similarly spoken of, though not mentioned by name, in the Book of Ezekiel, chapter 28. There it describes this "anointed cherub" (Ez. 28:13) as having a shining and extremely beautiful enjeweled body which possessed the ability to produce musical sounds or vibrations. His body was in fact his INSTRUMENT. This is explained in the following passage from Ezekiel:

> "...the workmanship of thy TABRETS and of thy PIPES was prepared IN THEE in the day thou wast created."
>
> Ezekiel 28:13

The word *tabret* means a tambourine or drum-type percussion instrument. The exact meaning of the word *pipes*, though a bit more obscure, is definitely connected in some way with the reproduction of sound: possibly vocal sound. So, in essence, what we are establishing is the fact that Lucifer was endowed with a God-given ability to create music and song.

At the advent of time, the music that this shining and beautiful angel produced gave glory to his Creator. It was music emanating directly from his pure, worshipful, and undefiled spirit.

Over a period of time, however, no one but God knows how long, Lucifer began a spiritual decline which was initially instigated by the simple act of self-aggrandizement. In other words, he became lifted up with PRIDE. His wisdom, intellect, beauty, and powers eventually became corrupted. His burgeoning pride resulted in spiritual SUICIDE. He gradually lost interest in the original purpose for his creation: to glorify God; choosing instead to use his radiant beauty and superior abilities to amass a following of his own. This self-patronizing, albeit unwise, decision alienated Lucifer from the TRUE source of his luminescence and life: his Holy and Perfect Creator. It was this irreversible act of rebellion against God's perfect will, which came to be known as "SIN", that finally caused Lucifer's expulsion from the heavenly Kingdom. Jesus, who personally witnessed this tragic occurrence, revealed the knowledge of this incident to His disciples. The record of this fateful moment in history is written in the Bible. He told them:

"I beheld Satan as lightning fall from heaven."

Luke 10:18

That is just a brief synopsis of the creation, life, and spiritual DEATH of the supernatural angelic being once known as Lucifer. Without the sustaining Life of God flowing within him, he became totally incapable of producing beauty or light. His musical abilities also suffered as a result of his fall.

Though he now exists in a fallen state, he has retained his musical aptitude. But in this day and age, he no longer depends on his own body for the creation of what is obviously a corrupt form of the original music he once produced. He makes most of his music now using *HUMAN* instruments: those people ready and willing to bargain away their eternal lives and souls in order to receive satanically endowed power, fortune, and fame. *THEY* are the *instruments* he now controls and PLAYS AT WILL.

If you look back for just a moment at the scripture that opened this chapter, you will find it contains a seemingly unusual statement. This prophetic scripture declares that people living at some time in the future will actually be *WORSHIP-ING* the DRAGON. But I guess, on second thought, that statement is really not that unusual. Why?? Because THEY ARE DOING IT NOW!!! The resurgence of the same satanism and devil worship, once strictly confined to isolated pagan cultures in obscure, out of the way places, is spreading dramatically across all quarters of the globe.

This same scripture also says people will be *WORSHIPING* the BEAST. Who or what is the Beast? The Bible states once again in the Book of the Revelation of Jesus Christ, that a man, whom God calls "THE BEAST", will suddenly arise from the sea of humanity and be given a great position of power by "the dragon". This event will occur during the last days of modern man and just preceding the establishment of God's Kingdom on Earth. The period of time when the Beast, who is also known as the anti- Christ, will reign is called the "TRIBULATION" period.

When the Beast first establishes his worldwide dominion, he will be donning the deceptive mask of a man of PEACE; but not long after his globally acclaimed inauguration the charade will end. In the short space of just a few years, his

4

once peaceful facade will quite unexpectedly dissolve away to reveal the TRUE face beneath: the grotesque visage of a tyrant with a propensity for DESTRUCTION AND WAR.

The reign of the Beast will explode into a ruthless and violent dictatorship, not unlike that of the infamous madman, ADOLF HITLER...but with one difference. Hitler was directly responsible for the annihilation of over six million Jews as well as untold numbers of God-fearing Christians; however, the anti- Christ will not just be killing a few million, he instead will be responsible for the deaths of HUNDREDS OF MILLIONS!!! This successor to Hitler known as the Beast (a name befitting him in every sense of the word) will have no qualms whatsoever about ordering the execution of *anyone* -- male, female, young, or old who will not worship him AS THEIR GOD. Thank God the anti-Christ forces will only reign for seven hellish years.

The Beast and his allied armies from every corner of the globe will find their ultimate defeat at the end of that seven year period on a crimson drenched battlefield in the middle- eastern valley of Megiddo. In our present day, many people are becoming more and more familiar with the name of this apocalyptic conflagration. Its name has become somewhat synonymous with the universal (though biblically inaccurate) concept of total world destruction. Laying aside the fact that it has an ancient Hebrew name, in our modern nuclear age we have, nevertheless, come to know it well, for it is *"called in the Hebrew tongue...* _ARMAGEDDON"_. (Rev. 16:16)

Indeed, all of this previously mentioned destruction is the sole responsibility of its initiator, the Dragon; because it is he who will give his unbridled, world-shaking power to the Beast. Question...What is the ultimate potential of the power at his disposal -- what kind of power does the Dragon actually wield? Answer...Prepare for a shock!

Recorded in the Book of Luke, chapter 4, is an encounter between Jesus and the Devil which took place in the Judean wilderness about 2000 years ago. This historic incident might give you a little insight into what kind of power the Dragon has. In verse 5 we are told that Satan actually had the incredible power to physically transport Jesus Christ, the Son of God, up onto a high mountain, where he also had the ability to produce before Him, in just a brief moment of time, a supernatural vision of all the kingdoms of the world. What the Devil then said to Jesus was an extremely revealing statement to anyone with ears to hear it. Satan said in verse 6:

> *"all this **POWER** will I GIVE THEE, and the glory of them* [ALL the world's kingdoms]: for that IS *DELIVERED UNTO ME; and to WHOMSOEVER I WILL I GIVE IT."*
>
> Luke 4:6

Now, do you fully understand the implications of that last statement made by the Devil? Because he already *OWNED* THIS ENTIRE WORLD SYSTEM and provided the power by which it ran, he was able to offer it *ALL* to Jesus!!! Have you ever wondered why things on this Earth are so corrupt, evil, and perverted? Now you **KNOW**. The world system in which we now live has always belonged to Satan.

Since Jesus Christ, Satan's adversary, was not interested in owning all, or any part of this contaminated world system, Satan had *NOTHING* to offer Him. Jesus dealt quickly and decisively with this satanic temptation. It had no effect on Him whatsoever. After Satan gave it his best shot, God the Son merely gave the royal command, *"BEGONE SATAN"*, and Satan fled the scene.

Jesus, already possessing universal omnipotence, was not even remotely interested in obtaining the powers of *this* world, but in our world today there are plenty of people who are.

The Dragon has been bestowing his power on, and infusing his heartbeat into, his followers since the beginning of time. Just as God anoints His faithful and obedient servants...Satan also anoints his.

From the downfall of this world system, which he craftily and strategically initiated, the Dragon has *ALWAYS* had this supernatural power to give. But the questions we now need to answer are, to whom would he give it, and *why*? We shall see...we shall see.

AND THEY WORSHIPED THE DRAGON

7

Siberian shaman holding his trance inducing drum. From the look on his face, you can see it must have worked well.

CHAPTER 2

THE SHAMAN'S DANCE

Throughout world history, civilizations from Babylon to Bangkok, from the Aztecs to the Aborigines, have always had what they referred to as their *"holy"* men. They are called shamans, witch doctors, medicine men, voodoo priests, sorcerers, yogis and a variety of other names and titles depending upon the nation or the culture. Regardless of what they are called, they all have basically the same task to perform. As the spiritual leaders of their societies, their chief responsibility is to bring their disciples, tribes, or cultures into a state of communion with the spirits in the unseen spirit world.

The position of shaman is always filled by a rather eccentric character, who through inheritance; a traumatic experience such as a severe illness; or a near-death accident, develops uncommon, otherworldly or psychic abilities which are recognized by the rest of the tribe. Many times a year the shaman will perform certain "magical" rituals for the benefit of the members of his tribe.

In almost all cases during the shamanic ritual, a drum beat of some type is used to induce a trance *STATE* in the shaman. The repetitive beat is a very effective tool used to bring about this altered state of consciousness, or *ecstatic state*. When this shift in consciousness occurs, contact with the spirit world is usually made.

The shaman will then begin to dance with these unseen spirit powers. Frequently this dancing in an ecstatic trance state will last for many hours. It is during this time that the spirits will come to commune with the shaman, often accompanying him on spiritual or astral journeys into other dimensions: some representing heaven, some representing hell. These journeys into the astral world can last anywhere from a few hours to many days.

The shamanic trance state will often be instigated or enhanced by the ingestion of narcotics. Ingestion of mind altering drugs, including tobacco (one shamanic drug whose use is very common in our western society today), is an integral part of the preparation the shaman undergoes enabling him to effectively commune with the spirit powers that are drawn to him by his evocative dance.

If the shaman is not careful and on guard at all times while in this ecstatic *STATE* (remember that word), spirit possession can, and often does, take place. Though most people fear even the possibility of witnessing an episode of demonic possession, let alone being possessed themselves, to many shamans, however, it is not necessarily looked upon as something to be feared. Some shamans actually seek this possession as a way of obtaining what they perceive as more spiritual power. The acquisition of power through possession is a concept many of them utilize and understand very well.

Now, what does all this information about shamans, drugs, and spirit possession have to do with Rock & Roll? More than you might think.

Most modern day singers in Rock & Roll are our present society's equivalent to tribal shamans.

One man in particular, who called himself "The Lizard King", not only accepted the role of shaman, but understood its true purpose. I would actually have to call him the founding father of Rock & Roll shamans. His name was Jim.

JIM MORRISON

"The shaman...he was a man who would intoxicate himself. See, he was probably already an ... uh ... unusual individual. And, he would put himself into a *trance* by dancing, whirling around, drinking, taking drugs--however. Then he would go on a mental travel and...uh...describe his journey to the rest of the tribe."[1]

JIM MORRISON - THE DOORS

It is obvious by that last quote from Jim Morrison he was well acquainted with the role of the shaman. I have personally watched him dancing and whirling around on stage lapsing into what could easily be described as a drug-induced trance state. Jim Morrison not only willingly identified with the mystical figure of the shaman, acknowledging and accepting the role as his own,

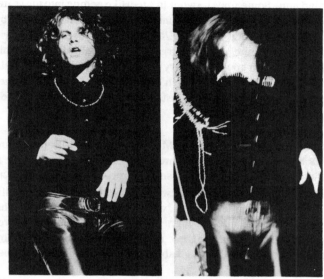

Lizard king shaman Jim Morrison photographed during one of his frequent trance dances.

but when this altered state would occur, his band, the Doors, was also aware of the transformation taking place.

From the Doors biography <u>No One Here Gets Out Alive</u>, keyboardist, Ray Manzarek knowingly explains:

"When the Siberian shaman gets ready to go into his trance all the villagers get together and shake rattles and blow whistles and play whatever instruments they have to send him off. There is a constant pounding, pounding, pounding. And these sessions last for hours. It was the same way with the Doors when we played in concert. The sets didn't last that long, but I think our drug experiences let us get into it that much quicker. We knew the symptoms of THE STATE [there's that word again!], so that we could try to approximate it. It was like Jim was an *ELECTRIC*

SHAMAN and we were the electric shaman's band pounding away behind him. Sometimes he wouldn't feel like getting into the **state**, but the band would keep on pounding and pounding, and little by little it would *TAKE HIM OVER*. God, I could send an electric shock through him with the organ. John could do it with his drumbeats. You could see every once in a while -twitch- I could hit a chord and make him twitch. And he'd be off again. Sometimes he was just incredible. Just amazing. And the audience felt it too!"[2]

As you can see, not only did Jim Morrison identify with the figure of the shaman, but his bandmate, Ray Manzarek, was also quite aware of the fact that being onstage with Jim *WAS* in every sense a true shamanic experience.

As we mentioned earlier, drugs also play a key role in the rituals of the shaman. The shamanic figure in India, who also uses intoxicants to enhance his spiritual experience, is called a yogi. An expert on comparative religions, Mircea Eliade, comments on this topic in his book entitled, Yoga: Immortality and Freedom. Concerning the drug habits of the yogis and shamans he states:

"As for ritual intoxication by hemp, opium, and other narcotics, it is a practice abundantly attested in the shamanic world as well as among some yogins...in fact a certain number of saktas and members of other ecstatic and orgiastic movements used and STILL USE OPIUM AND HASHISH."[3]

Curiously enough, not only have narcotics played a major role in tantric yoga and shamanic rituals, but they have also been an integral part of the celebration of Rock & Roll.

The very same drugs (marijuana, opium, hashish, etc.) that are used by the yogis and shamans are the same ones that began flooding the Rock & Roll stages and concert halls of the American landscape in the 1960's and 70's. Once again, this in no coincidence.

Sexually explicit behavior (very popular in Rock & Roll) is often also included by the yogi or shaman during the ritual or dance. These sexual encounters can either be experienced in the visible, physical realm with one or more persons in participation (group sex -- commonly called an orgy), or **they can** be experienced *totally* in the invisible spirit realm with only the shaman and the spirit or spirits he has summoned taking part. As far as the shaman is concerned, in either case, whether their partner is in the visible or invisible realm, the *coition does take place.*

Lead vocalists, both male and female, throughout the history of contemporary Rock & Roll, have often described having these very same overpowering *SEXUAL* feelings as well as *ORGIASTIC* experiences *DURING THEIR PERFORMANCES!* Here are just a few quotes from some of the more well known singers which might help to explain what I mean:

"I like to think that people go away knowing that we're pretty raunchy and we really do a lot of the things people say we do...I like them to go away feeling the way you do after a good chick, satisfied and exhausted...some nights I just look out there and want to f__k the whole first row."[4]

ROBERT PLANT - LED ZEPPELIN

"I play the role of being a rock star on stage. When the music works, the audience and the performer often feel like they're having an ORGASM together."[5]

JOHN TAYLOR - DURAN DURAN

"I get a strange feeling on stage. I feel all this energy coming from the audience. They need something from life and are trying to get it from us. I often want to smash the microphone up because I don't feel the same person onstage as I am normally. I entice the audience...what I'm doing is a *sexual thing.* I dance, and all dancing is a replacement for sex."[6]

MICK JAGGER - ROLLING STONES

"When I look into the eyes of the audience and I know they're getting off on my music, I feel like I can perform all night. At times like that, I truly feel like I'm making love to my entire audience."[7]

PAT BENATAR

That last quote was from a woman. Though it is more of a rarity, women can also assume the role of shaman. Is Pat Benatar an isolated case in her expression of these erotic feelings? Not at all. Here are just a few more comments from some of the other ladies of Rock & Roll, describing, once again, these same shamanic sexual feelings:

> "The stage is our bed, and the audience is our broad, we're not entertaining - **we're making love.**"[8]
> GRACE SLICK - JEFFERSON AIRPLANE

> "I've always thought the main ingredients in rock are sex, really good stage shows, and really sassy music. Sex and sass. I just dance around and shake. **ROCK & ROLL IS ALL SEX. 100%. Sometimes music can make you *come*.**"[9] (slang term for achieving orgasm)
> DEBBIE HARRY - BLONDIE

> "Every time we play I have **ORGASMS** - especially on 'Butcher Baby'."[10] (title of a Plasmatics song)
> WENDY O. WILLIAMS - PLASMATICS

All of these aforementioned singers either attribute their orgasmic experiences to the music they are producing or their desire to intimately interact with their audience, but could these sexual feelings originate from another source? I believe they do.

In a book entitled, <u>Ecstatic Religion: A Study of Shamanism and Spirit Possession</u>, an explanation is given for what is possibly happening during this shamanic experience. You may not only find it interesting, but shocking as well. What about the sexual feelings that all these Rock & Roll singers are experiencing? Do they get these orgiastic feelings from the music *OR* are they actually being stimulated by their possessing spirits? Here is what the book <u>Ecstatic Religion</u> by author I.M. Lewis declares regarding this experience.

Black Sabbath album cover "Sabbath Bloody Sabbath" depicting a spiritual seduction of a man by incubi and succubi demonic spirits.

"...ecstatic POSSESSION SEIZURES are sometimes, explicitly interpreted as acts of **MYSTICAL SEXUAL INTERCOURSE** between the subject [the shaman] and his or her possessing spirit."[11]

Possession seizures -- **sexual intercourse** with spirits? Does the bizarre concept of having a *SEXUAL ENCOUNTER WITH DEMONS* sound incredulous? Well, believe it or not, in Witchcraft, Shamanism, Satanism, and many other forms of sorcery, IT HAPPENS. If the sexual spirit impersonates or takes on the characteristics of a female it is called a SUCCUBUS; the male impersonating counterpart is called an INCUBUS. In either case, male or female, the encounter is accompanied by actual physical sensations.

In his book, I.M. Lewis also quotes Earnest Jones, author of the book, <u>On The Nightmare</u>, as observing quite matter of factly "that 'sexual intercourse can occur between mortals and supernatural beings is one of the most widespread of human beliefs'". An example of a visual depiction of such an encounter is displayed on the cover of the Black Sabbath album entitled, "Sabbath Bloody Sabbath". In this picture you will see a man being surrounded by both male (incubi) and female (succubi) impersonating (familiar) spirits who are in the process of procuring his seduction.

Satanist, musician, and ritual magician, Nicholas Schreck, an official spokesperson for the Church of Satan, knows personally of these seducing spirits. He has recorded an album which contains musical compositions consisting of frequencies and modulations that are specifically created for the unique purpose of *drawing* these sexual demons into the presence of the listener. Schreck, however, is not the only one who has recorded music specifically designed to produce this result. Many Rock & Roll musicians write songs that do exactly the same thing.

There have been a number of other books throughout history, besides the ones we have already mentioned, that discuss what the rational mind would normally consider to be the highly unusual practice of spirit cohabitation. However, this practice is considered quite normal and often even necessary in the life of a shaman. Some shamans even go so far as to *MARRY* their male or female possessing spirit. Though you may find this information incomprehensible, if not totally inconceivable, a sexual relationship with a spirit can frequently be an integral part of the complete shamanic experience.

Now, the next time you see a lead vocalist moving *sexually* to the hypnotic beat of the music, remember all the information you just read. Some lead singers, as you watch them perform (just as in the films of shamans I have observed), seem to suddenly lose all their inhibitions and control, and begin moving with a pelvic thrusting gesture. In the case of the Rock & Roll singer, this gesture is done with either their instrument, their mike stand, a stage prop (mannequin, blow-up doll, female dancer, etc.), the floor of the stage itself, or the air. It is as though they are fornicating with an invisible partner. Far from this sexual display being just a part of the act, there could be quite a different reason for their erotic behavior. Could they, like the shamans, actually be having spiritual intercourse with their possessing spirit?? Something interesting to consider, isn't it?

I have personally witnessed many singers perform this pelvic thrusting gesture. Here are just a few whose names might sound familiar: Mick Jagger, Jim Morrison, David Bowie, Elvis Presley, Burton Cummings (the Guess Who),

Perry Farrell (Jane's Addiction), George Michael, Adam Ant, Prince, Robert Plant, Steven Tyler (Aerosmith), Billy Idol, David Lee Roth, W. Axl Rose (Guns 'n' Roses), Rod Stewart, Alice Cooper, Jimi Hendrix, Anthony Kiedis (Red Hot Chili Peppers), Ian Astbury (The Cult), and Brett Michaels (Poison). Also, singers like Michael & Janet Jackson, Paula Abdul, Madonna, Bobby Brown, The New Kids On The Block, and rappers such as The Beastie Boys, M.C. Hammer, Tone Loc, 2 Live Crew, and many others too numerous to mention exhibit this same sexual movement in their *dancing*. Is there really any difference? Just take a close look at the expression on their faces and you will definitely see the evidence of *something spiritual taking place*. Could they, as well, actually be having sexual encounters with possessing demon spirits? Well, think about it for a minute. Since SHAMANS *DO*, I would dare to say, that is one possibility that must be considered.

Now you might, however, want to argue that these singers are not personally aware of any such possession taking place; but that, as we will presently see, is not always the case.

David Lee Roth, former lead singer for the rock supergroup, Van Halen, and now fronting his own group, not only acknowledges these sexual feelings, but their demonic spirit source as well. He says:

> "Whatever your vice, whatever somebody else can't do in his 9 to 5 job, I can do in rock & roll. When I'm on stage, my basement facilities [i.e. his sexual desires] take over completely. When I'm on stage it's like **doing it with 20,000 of your closest friends.**"[12]

There, once again is the evidence of the sexual feelings; but what about his awareness of their demonic source? Let's let David tell us himself. He says:

> "I'm going to abandon myself to them, which is what I attempt to do. You work yourself into that **STATE** and you fall in SUPPLI-CATION OF **THE DEMON GODS.**"[13]

Now not only do we hear about the demon gods to whom he is subservient, but once again you also hear that word which describes the spiritual condition of the possessed shaman: the *STATE*.

David Lee Roth is not the only lead singer to admit to an understanding of the demonic source of his musical powers. Marc Storace, the lead vocalist for the rock group Krokus also knows the source of his inspiration. He says:

"You can't describe it except to say it's like a mysterious energy that comes *INTO MY BODY*. It's almost like BEING A *ME-DIUM*."[14]

Though in that last statement he avoids identifying this "mysterious energy" as demonic, in another quote from this same man, we can clearly see he *truly* understands what is taking place. He says:

"If you bring them in, if you ALLOW THEM *ENTRANCE*, if you allow yourself to *meditate with the DARK POWERS*, and through yourself, let them be seen, they will be seen and people will respond to them."[15]

It seems quite clear by the last few quotes that at least *some* lead singers *KNOW* that they are being possessed and used as MEDIUMS for the DARK POWERS.

The shaman, the Rock & Roll singer, the trance-dancer, the medium, are all victims of the force behind the music. The forces that electrify, drive, motivate, and frequently *possess* many Rock & Roll musicians are as old as the ages. Many, many more examples could have been given, but suffice it to say that an intriguing pattern is developing...and the surprises are only just beginning.

CHAPTER 3

TO POSSESS A RACE

In my search to understand the origin and purpose of Rock & Roll I have discovered evidence which clearly exposes an incredible interconnectedness between Rock & Roll, Hinduism, Shamanism, Satanism, and Voodoo which has both startled and intrigued me. It is a fact that whenever I have researched any two or more of these subjects simultaneously, I have consistently found proof of an underlying spiritual force responsible for their operation. On the surface, these ideologies may seem to be quite diverse but deep within their core they are unmistakably identical. Let's dig a little deeper now and further establish our foundation.

In the February 12, 1976 issue of *Rolling Stone* magazine is an interview featuring bisexual musician, singer, actor, song writer, performer, and occultist David Bowie. The message that Bowie shared with the readers of Rolling Stone was at the least, very revealing. Concerning the subject of Rock & Roll, David Bowie made these statements:

> "Rock has always been the Devil's music. You can't convince me that it isn't...I believe that rock & roll is dangerous. It could well bring about a very evil feeling in the west...That's where I see it heading, bringing about the dark era...I feel that we're only heralding something even *darker than ourselves.*"[1]

As you just read, David Bowie truly believed that the Rock & Roll he played was just a harbinger of the ultimate darkness to come; the music itself being just a forerunner, if you will, of the response it would incite within the heart of our society. Could Bowie have been inadvertently prophesying the rise in the incidents of satanic crime, human sacrifice, and the practicing of all types of occultism that we have witnessed within the last thirty years? Good question.

Well, I'm not exactly in the habit of accepting prophecy from rock stars, but what Bowie stated back in 1976 has proven to be frighteningly accurate; as here in the 1990's we have already seen, and continue to see, the Devil's darkness growing by leaps and bounds. It is quite evident today that our Rock & Roll society, as Bowie foretold, is indeed in a state of spiritual disintegration. Yes, David Bowie's prediction was essentially correct, but it came a little too late to be considered a true revelation. By the time David made his debut in 1967, the occult connection with the dark era of Rock & Roll he had foreseen had already been made by some of Britain's other musicians, who during their heyday, had already made their contacts, or should I say *contracts*, with the Evil One (this will be discussed in a later chapter).

Way back in the early 1950's, however, on a different continent, an astonishing albeit extremely revealing incident had already taken place. On a video tape dealing with the subject of Rock & Roll and the occult, Rev. Gary Greenwald of Eagles Nest Ministries in California relates a very unusual occurrence that had been witnessed during a church service in a small town in Canada. According to Rev. Greenwald's account, a young girl who had been continually subjecting herself to a steady diet of the earliest Rock & Roll (the so-called "safe stuff") was attending the service and quite unexpectedly began to twist and writhe around on the floor hissing like a snake. Suddenly, a voice which was not her own came out of her mouth proclaiming itself as a powerful prince of darkness. When the church's pastor commanded the spirit to reveal its actual identity, the one possessing the girl said:

> "I'm a prince and I'm coming down...we're all coming down...to possess a race, the YOUTH OF THIS LAND!"

The statement made that night by the demonic principality, who had gained entry into and was now in possession of the girl, turned out to be no idle threat. It seemed that the powers of darkness planned to use Rock & Roll to accomplish their goal of dominating the youth. Almost overnight, many Rock & Roll musicians began a marked rise in popularity and prestige within the entertainment world. All across the continent, Rock & Roll became a powerful and controlling force that had to be acknowledged.

Many preachers who quickly recognized the dangers of this new spiritual threat and attempted to expose it were laughed at, mocked, chided, and ridiculed by the general public for calling Rock & Roll "the Devil's music". The public should have listened, because according to the testimony of David Bowie, one of the most popular and prestigious musicians of our time...the preachers were right.

Now, just as in any other political, social, or religious movement in history there are the faithful who comprise the backbone of the organization. Rock & Roll also had its hard working founders. Let's just see on what type of foundation it was built.

ELVIS

One of the true fathers of the movement was a young kid from a pentecostal Christian background who would become known as the king of Rock & Roll. His name was Elvis Presley.

Elvis Aron Presley was born January 8, 1935 in the little town of Tupelo, Mississippi. From his earliest years all the way through his teens, he was constantly exposed to the Bible. Although he attended a Christian church, the

Elvis pictured with occult friend and mentor, Larry Geller, not long before Elvis' death.

First Assembly of God, regularly, he never totally committed himself to the Christian faith.

Though in his rebellious youth he did not choose to receive Christ, God did not abandon Elvis. One day as he was riding in his limousine, he saw a man standing on a street corner preaching the Gospel. Elvis had seen this street preacher before, and somewhere deep down inside, he knew he was a man of God. He invited him to come to Graceland for a meeting where they could talk in-depth without interruption. The preacher readily accepted the invitation. Elvis had many questions regarding spiritual matters and they talked for a long time. The most pressing question, however, on the mind of Elvis Presley dealt with the issue of eternal salvation. He wanted to know what he needed to do to be saved. The man God sent to Presley told him that if he truly wanted salvation he would have to become a born-again Christian and give his entire life unreservedly to Jesus Christ. There was no other way to be saved. The preacher then offered to lead him in a prayer to receive Jesus Christ as his Lord and Savior, but Elvis wavered. He told the man that if he were to become born-again he felt he would not even be able to *play* the Rock & Roll music he loved, let alone sing some of his lyrics. Elvis knew deep within his heart God would never approve of his present career, so with some reluctance he made his decision. With this decision to forgo the salvation prayer made, and having nothing left to discuss with him, the preacher then prayed for Elvis and left...Presley remained unsaved. Elvis Presley freely chose to turn his back on Christ at that crucial meeting. He chose Rock & Roll instead.

As a result of that decision, Elvis opened a door to occult influence that would radically change and totally consume the rest of his life. He opted for a more permissive and compromising spirituality that would allow him to continue to play his Rock & Roll, instead of a spirituality based on Truth.

One day, through that open door into Elvis' soul walked an occultist named Larry Geller. Geller, who was hired as Elvis' hairdresser, became his close friend and confidant as well as his mentor. He initiated Elvis into deeper aspects of the occult and together they traveled down the spiritual path of darkness. Elvis had many deceptive spiritual experiences on that path; some of them eventually even leading him to believe, not that he should *serve* Jesus Christ, but that HE *WAS* JESUS CHRIST!

A large trunk full of New Age/occult books became his constant companion. He became absorbed in the study of a multitude of esoteric religions, two of them being Rosicrucianism and Theosophy. Both of these belief systems find their roots in Hinduism.

Everyone close to Elvis Presley knew he was on a constant search for two things in his life: PEACE and TRUTH. Had he gone back to his spiritual roots and turned to the REAL Jesus Christ, his search for meaning would have ended in victory. Unfortunately, he did not.

True Christianity and Rock & Roll do not mix; Elvis knew it and made his choice.

Bloated, drug-addicted, depressed, and deceived, the king of Rock & Roll died of what has been reported as advanced arteriosclerosis or, to put in less medical terms, heart failure. On August 16, 1977, his earthly journey came to an abrupt end. Later published reports regarding his death, however, have even intimated suicide by drug overdose. Whatever the cause of his decease may have been, one thing is painfully clear; the Dragon's brand of "truth" which Elvis had chosen to embrace had ultimately taken its inevitable and final toll.

The tragic story of Elvis Presley, however, may actually have a happy ending. It is rumored that Presley finally accepted Jesus as his personal Savior just before his death. I sincerely hope for his sake this rumor is true. Someday we will all find out for sure.

JERRY LEE LEWIS

Many people, besides Elvis Presley, have been responsible for promoting this rising force called Rock & Roll; but some of these people have played more of a key role in its promotion than others. One such man is Jerry Lee Lewis.

Jerry Lee Lewis was born September 29, 1935 in Ferriday, Louisiana. Just like Elvis, who was coincidentally born the same year, he was also from a Christian background. However, there was one big problem in the spiritual life of the Lewis family -- alcohol. Jerry Lee's father, Elmo, was *not* a Christian, he was a MOONSHINER, who, because of his illegal occupation of operating a still, was caught, convicted, and subsequently incarcerated for a time in the New Orleans Federal Jail. Not long after his release Jerry Lee was born. Just like his father Elmo, he also became involved with moonshine; not necessarily making it, but definitely *drinking* it.

23

On more than one occasion, young Jerry Lee felt the sting of "white lightning". He fondly reminisces of his father's homemade brew:

> "He made the best whiskey I ever tasted, drunk it all the time. Whiskey's good if you drink it right and I never knew any other way to drink it."[2]

One of the best ways to become demon possessed is through alcohol. Unfortunately for him, Jerry Lee Lewis' early experience with moonshine made him a prime candidate.

As a young boy, Jerry Lee and his cousins, Mickey Gilley, and Jimmy Swaggert, would sneak down to a black honkytonk called Haney's Big House where they would sit outside the club for hours listening to the musicians play their rockin' boogie and blues. This is where Jerry Lee Lewis' interest in Rock & Roll began.

This alcohol and narcotic inspired music that saturated his soul during the early years of his life had an indelible and lasting effect on young Jerry Lee. He was addicted.

Despite being sent to Southwestern Bible Institute in Waxahachie, Texas, at the tender age of fifteen, it soon became apparent that the music on which he had been weaned had a stranglehold on his life that would not let go. Even while at the school, he tried entertaining the other boys with his frenzied, boogie-style music on the piano. All this succeeded in doing was getting him expelled.

From there it was only a short step back into darkness and onto the Rock & Roll stages of America where the audiences would be delighted to have him play the raucous music that he loved. They would even pay him to do it.

He, like Elvis, made his choice between God and Rock & Roll. God came in second.

Jerry Lee also knew the source of his "talent". He spoke about it very candidly during a recording session at Sam Phillips' Sun Studios. He told Sam:

> "Man I got the *Devil in me*. If I didn't have I'd be a Christian."[3]

Though he often suffered internal conflict and guilt as a result of his Christian roots, it seems he knew his true spiritual condition quite well.

The devils which had taken up residence in him early in his life quickly elevated him to super-stardom. His name became one of the most powerful drawing cards in the business. The young rockin' rebels, the aficionados of this crazy beat showed up in droves to watch him bang out manic Rock & Roll masterpieces on his heavily abused ivories. For a while he was a true champion for the cause of Rock & Roll and a prime recipient of the Dragon's blessings -- but then quite suddenly, as can be the case when dealing with the Dragon, things changed. The Devil raised him up...and then, without warning, the same Devil knocked him down.

After the dissolution of two marriages, the first lasting one year, the second lasting four, his third marriage was to one of his own relatives: his third cousin, Myra Brown. She was only 13 years old at the time. This action totally outraged many of his loyal fans and completely alienated him from the entire country of England. Instead of enthusiastically welcoming his tour, they chided, derided, and *expelled* him.

Not long afterward, his Rock & Roll kingdom came down with a crash. Concert promoters who previously begged him to perform in their halls would no longer book him. The once promising career of wildman Jerry Lee Lewis came to a screeching halt.

With his world coming apart at the seams, he found solace in his only loyal friend -- alcohol. His excessive drinking slowly began to take its toll.

Tragedy began to follow him around like the plague. In 1962, his son Steve drowned. In 1973, his other son was killed in an automobile accident. In 1976, Lewis even shot his bass player in the chest (or arm, depending on which account you read).

Not only was his life filled with misery and tragedy, but the Grim Reaper was also hot on his heels. In 1981, both his life and his health hit rock bottom. He was admitted to a hospital in Memphis, Tennessee, and after two operations on a perforated stomach ulcer, pneumonia set in. He was given only a 5% chance of survival.

Just before his emergency hospitalization and abdominal surgery, Jerry Lee had the good sense to call out to God for forgiveness so, just in case he didn't make it through the operation, he would not spend eternity in hell. That was a very good move on his part. He recalled the incident in an interview conducted not long ago with *SPIN* magazine:

"I thought I was dead, as a matter of fact. I knew that it was over for me. When I hit the floor and my stomach split open, I had enough sense to get my house in order with God...Son, it's the strangest feeling looking in the bathroom mirror and watching your stomach split open. I thought, you're going to die Jerry Lee, maybe you're already dead. So I started praying, I asked God to forgive me of all of my sins. 'Cause I knew that I'd done wrong and that I was going to hell. If there is a hell then I don't even want to be close to it, and if there is no hell, if there's only a heaven, I don't want to take no chances. It is for eternity, they say."[4]

In the same interview, Jerry Lee publicly expressed his regrets for not having lived his life in service to Jesus Christ and choosing Rock & Roll as his god instead. He also told *SPIN* magazine:

"That's what I should be doing, that's my first love, I think. Do you think it's what I'll have to go back to? I think I probably will. I'm talking about my belief in God, in the Son of God, the Holy Ghost and the Gospel. I think I'll have to go back and straighten my life up and do it right. Really do it right not just talk about it...The greatest honor that a person can have in this life is to be a fully-fledged Christian..."[5]

Now, that sounds like another very wise decision. However, with the recent release of the new movie, "Great Balls of Fire", based on his life story (now available on video), and his regenerated popularity, it doesn't appear he's in a very big hurry to get right with God.

What he really needs to do is repent, renounce his past, and be renewed in CHRIST. I earnestly pray to God that he does.

From the very beginning of his Rock & Roll career, Jerry Lee knew, just as Elvis did, that his music was straight from the Devil. It seems he has yet to be willing to change his tune.

Jerry Lee Lewis, to this day, can still be heard in the Rock & Roll halls of America, singing the line to a song he made famous -- "Goodness, gracious, great balls of fire." However, he needs to realize for his own sake, it is only

GOD'S goodness and *graciousness* that is still keeping a lost, dying, and unrepentant soul named Jerry Lee Lewis from the real "great balls of FIRE".

LITTLE RICHARD

Another piano pounding father of early Rock & Roll to come from a Christian background is Richard Penniman, or as he is better known around the world, Little Richard.

Every major figure of any prominence in the realm of Rock & Roll credits Little Richard as their main inspiration; and as far as the dispute over who is the true king of Rock & Roll, the decision is unanimous. A list of those who desired to walk in his flamboyant footsteps reads like a list of Who's Who in the history of Rock & Roll: Elvis Presley, Mick Jagger, John Lennon, Paul McCartney, Elton John, Jimi Hendrix, David Bowie, Sam Cooke, Bo Diddley, Janis Joplin, Screaming Lord Sutch, Gene Vincent, Buddy Holly, Chuck Berry, James Brown, Smokey Robinson, Pat Boone, and Otis Redding just to mention a few.

He is constantly showered with accolades by many professional Rock & Roll musicians of today. Here are just some of the praises they sing for their Rock & Roll king:

Mick Jagger of the Rolling Stones said:

"I'd heard so much about the audience reaction that I thought there must be some exaggeration. But it was all true. He drove the whole house into a complete frenzy. There's no single phrase to describe his hold on the audience. It might excite some and terrify others. It's *HYPNOTIC,* like an evangelistic meeting where, for want of a better phrase, Richard is the disciple and the audience is the flock that follows. I couldn't believe the power of Little Richard on stage. He was amazing. Chuck Berry is my favorite, along with Bo, but nobody could beat Little Richard's stage act. Little Richard is the originator and my first idol."[6]

Jon Lord, the keyboardist for Deep Purple said:

"There would have been no Deep Purple if there had been no Little Richard."[7]

Paul Simon, of Simon and Garfunkel fame, said:

"When I was in High School I wanted to be like Little Richard."[8]

Marty Balin of the Jefferson Airplane said:

"Little Richard, was the God. I grew up on Little Richard in the rockin' fifties."[9]

Otis Redding said:

"If it hadn't been for Little Richard I would not be here. I entered the music business because of Richard -- he is my inspiration."[10]

John Lennon said:

"Elvis was bigger than religion in my life. Then this boy at school said he'd got this record by somebody called Little Richard who was better than Elvis -- I didn't want to leave Elvis, but this was so much better."[11]

Smokey Robinson said:

"Little Richard is the beginning of Rock & Roll."[12]

Well maybe Little Richard wasn't exactly the beginning of Rock & Roll, as we will shortly discover, but it is true that he ignited a fire with his music that has yet to be extinguished. One would probably be safe in saying he was the match that lit the inferno and sent it raging out of control.

above: *Little Richard the early years . . . The Esquerita look alike.*
below: *Little Richard's gay and flambouyant mentor, Esquerita. Notice the distinct similarity in the make-up and hairstyle.*

What was the private life of this idolized innovator actually like?...Filled with homosexuality, drugs, and perversion. Let's just say the demons of lust and excess had another willing soul in which to take up residence.

He began his practice of homosexuality at a very young age as a result of (what I have gathered through my research as) the feelings he experienced after receiving a french kiss from a gay man. That was just the beginning. He soon began hanging around the all night restaurant at the Macon, Georgia Greyhound Bus Station looking for sex. One night while he was "cruising" he met an effeminate musician named Esquerita. That night he not only had his desire for gay sex fulfilled, but he also had his first lesson in how to play Rock & Roll piano. It seems this homosexual piano player is the person who turned Little Richard on...in more ways than one. (Unfortunately for him, Eskew Reeder, aka Esquerita, is no longer able to enjoy his homosexual encounters, or his Rock & Roll. He died of AIDS on October 23, 1986.)

As Little Richard's Rock & Roll career began to bloom, so did his insatiable desire for perversion. He would actually pay men and women to have sex in front of him so he could sit and watch. He remembers:

> "I used to watch these people having sex with my band men. I would pay a guy who had a big penis to come and have sex with these ladies so I could watch them. It was a big thrill for me.. As I was watching I would masturbate..."[13]

Another of his favorite perversions was watching lesbian sexual encounters.

In the Bible, God gives a label to such illicit sexual behavior; God's Word calls it *"vile affections"*. The Bible states:

> *"...God gave them up unto vile affections: for even their women did change the natural use into that which is **against** **nature**: And likewise also the men, leaving the natural use of the woman, burned in their lust one toward another; men with men working that which is **unseemly**..."*
>
> Romans 1:26,27

In the Old Testament God labeled homosexuality an abomination punishable by death (Lev. 20:13).

Little Richard was also once arrested for driving around town with a half-naked girl in the backseat of his car giving invitations for people to climb in and "enjoy" her. His life was one big perverted *ORGY*. With Little Richard it didn't matter whether it was sex with men, women, or BOTH. His body and soul became a welcome home for any number of wayfaring unclean spirits. Without a doubt, he was **possessed**.

You rarely find perverted sex without illicit drugs and Little Richard was no exception. Drugs of all types were flowing freely in his sordid life. Alcohol, PCP (angel dust), heroin, marijuana, and especially cocaine were some of his favorites. He even experimented with LSD.

Everyone who knew him knew that he had power; power to control an audience and literally drive them into a frenzy. Girls in the audience would become so sexually stimulated by his performance they would actually tear off their underwear and throw it at the stage.

Oh yes, this Rock & Roll "king" knew he had power, but he also knew it didn't come from him. He was fully aware that he was wielding a power which was controlled by the forces of darkness. In a book based on his life story, Little Richard candidly reveals the source of his power:

> "...I was directed and commanded by another power. The power of darkness. The power that you've heard so much about. The power that a lot of people don't believe exists. The power of the Devil. Satan. We must realize there's a force that is fighting against us in this world."[14]

Living the life of Rock & Roll, naturally Richard personally knew many other musicians in the business. Some of those he met knew more about this "power" than most people would suspect. Only an insider like Little Richard could have been privy to what was going on behind the scenes, but there were certain groups he was aware of who were actually participating in DEVIL WORSHIP. He once told a reporter from the Harrisburg Patriot News:

"Some rock and roll groups stand around in a circle and drink cups of *blood;* some get on their knees and pray to the *DEVIL.* Rock and roll hypnotizes us and controls our senses."[15]

I think by the last quote from Little Richard, one who has walked the same path, you can see that not *all* the groups who have exploited the concept of the "satanic" in their music and public image are just playacting opportunists. Some of them are serious, demonized BELIEVERS.

It is without question, Little Richard *knew* that Rock & Roll was the Dragon's progeny.

Though he periodically confesses Jesus Christ as his Savior, at last count Little Richard is once again back on that same old Rock & Roll road.

In a very recent issue of *Rolling Stone* magazine, a recent appearance on the Arsenio Hall show, as well as a cameo appearance in a rock video produced by the band Cinderella (where Richard poses as a telephone operator receiving pledges for a fundraiser to promote and save Rock & Roll), we once again find him willing to sell his soul to be known as the *KING* of Rock & Roll. *Pride* is one of the Dragon's most powerful and deceptive snares, and in Richard Penniman's case it could be his downfall. I would advise Richard, and anyone else reading this book, not to be too concerned about being known as a king. The only king who will be receiving eternal worship and glory is the "King of Kings", Jesus Christ. Every other king will someday be bowing his knee to Him.

My advice to Richard Penniman: Friend, let go of your "old man" and turn back to the Gospel before the door of your repetitiously seared conscience closes for good. God loves you...but He doesn't love Rock & Roll, and as you well know, *never did.* You may want your own crown, but remember, all earthly crowns will quickly perish when they enter into "the Lake of FIRE".

CONCLUSION OF CHAPTER

Now what exactly have we found out in this chapter? Elvis Presley, Jerry Lee Lewis, and Little Richard, three of the fathers of Rock & Roll, were all exposed to the truth of the Bible and all came from Christian backgrounds. When they decided to walk away from God they automatically joined the losing team. Elvis ended up thinking he *was* Jesus Christ; Jerry Lee Lewis very nearly ended up dead; and little Richard, because of his desire for notoriety, still fluctuates between confession and confusion.

Their individual and personal experiences may have been different but there was one observation they all shared in common. As we have already discovered by their own admission, they each *KNEW* their music was completely controlled by the Devil. So, you can clearly see, the power behind three of the earliest Rock & Roll fathers was unquestionably forged in the fires of Hell; but the story doesn't end here...

Though there is much more that could be said about the anti- Christ spirit of rebellion in the earliest days of Rock & Roll, it's now time to shift our attention to the excavation of its occult roots and discover how they became so firmly implanted, sinking their dark tendrils of demonic influence deep into the fertile minds of the young, in those "innocent" early days I call the *birthpangs of the Dragon's NEW child*.

Heartbeat of the Dragon

CHAPTER 4

VOODOO CHILDREN

"Well I'm a VOODOO CHILD
Lord I'm a voodoo child
The night I was born
Lord, I swear the moon turned a fire red...
My poor mother cried out now the gypsy was right
And I seen her fell down right dead...
'Cause I'm a voodoo child
Lord knows, I'm a voodoo child..."

VOODOO CHILD - JIMI HENDRIX

Voodoo, a rather clandestine religion finding most of its ancient roots in the Yoruba culture of Africa, is today mainly associated with the geographical locations of Jamaica, Haiti, and South America. It is a belief system primarily involved with the worship of pagan gods and goddesses -- spirits with names such as: Agwe -- the spirit of the sea, Damballah Wedo -- the serpent god, and Erzulie -- the spirit of love. These deities are known as the *loa*.

The Haitian peasants who are predominantly the ones (though definitely not the only ones) who practice the religion of Vodoun, more commonly referred to as Voodoo, live their lives in absolute servitude to their gods. They understand and readily acknowledge their complete dependence upon these deities for protection, guidance, prosperity, and even personal health. They have said, concerning these spirits they worship:

"The loa love us, protect us, and guard us. They tell us what is happening to our relations who live far away, they suggest to us remedies which bring us relief when we are sick...If we are hungry the loa appear to us in a dream and say 'Take courage: you will earn money' and the promised money comes."[1]

Not only do these gods protect, inform, and heal their servants, sometimes upon request, the loa will even *KILL* their enemies for them.

As far as the followers of this religion are concerned, their worship of these spirit gods and goddesses is totally legitimate. The celebrants of Voodoo say: *One either serves the loa or one does not.*

SERPENTS AND RAINBOWS

Many people still speculate about the existence of this strange religion. Let's let one who has observed it firsthand take us a step beyond speculation and be our expert witness.

In 1974, anthropologist, biologist, and explorer Wade Davis began an investigation, a search for the truth about Voodoo. His adventures invariably led to the authoring of one of the most incredibly detailed eyewitness accounts ever written concerning the Vodoun religion. The book, which was a best-seller and made its debut in 1985, was entitled, The Serpent and The Rainbow. It received even more publicity, however, when the story was made into a blockbuster hit movie of the same name.

Whether through the unusual accounts written about in the book or the dramatic occult imagery depicted in the movie, it can undoubtedly be ascertained that Wade Davis did experience the reality of Voodoo. He has seen their celebrations...He has also watched the loa *possess* them. He writes of one such celebration where he witnessed the natives gathered to worship the god Ogoun, the spirit of fire and war. He recalls:

"Around the periphery of the basin a ring of candles burns for the spirit, and the pilgrims dressed in bright cotton lean precariously over the mud to leave offerings of rum and meat, rice and wine. There is a battery of drums to one side, and those mounted by the spirit enter the basin, disappear, and emerge *transformed*. One sees a young man, his body submerged with only his eyes showing, move steadily like a reptile past the legs of naked women, their

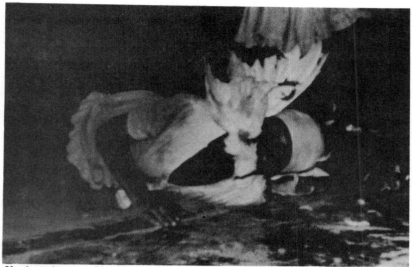

Voodoo priestess or Mambo possessed by the loa accepts and partakes in the blood sacrifice. She is biting the head off a live chicken.

skin coated with slimy clay...At the base of the mapou [tree], Ogoun feeds leaves and rum to a sacrificial bull; others reach out to touch it, and then the machete cuts into its throat, and the blood spreads over the surface of the mud. I was watching all this when I felt something fluid -- not water or sweat or rum -- trickle down my arm. I turned to a man pressed close beside me and saw his arm, riddled with needles and small blades, and the blood running copiously over the scars of past years, staining some leaves bound to his elbow before dripping from his skin to mine. The man was smiling. He too was *POSSESSED*, like the youth straddling the dying bull, or the dancers and the women wallowing in the mud."[2]

This Voodoo celebration witnessed by Davis was not only punctuated by wild erratic dancing, blood sacrifice, and self-mutilation, but, as you have read in the last quote, in this pagan religion the climax of the worship ceremony *always* involves *POSSESSION*.

Yes, my friends, Voodoo is quite REAL. Wade Davis, as well as many others whose writings I have read, have witnessed the celebration of this dark religion of blood, fire, drugs, sex, and demonic possession.

But what does Voodoo have to do with Rock & Roll? You are about to find out. Call it Voodoo, call it Voudoun, call it Tantra, call it Santeria, call it Candomblé, call it Macumba, call it Satanism, call it Shamanism, or even call it *Rock & Roll*; with a close, in-depth investigation, surprisingly enough, you will find an uncanny similarity in them all. They all have something to do with a beat, controlling powers or spirit forces, sacrifice (literal or symbolic), ceremonial dancing, music, and worship.

You just might be saying right now, 'How could you include Rock & Roll among all those strange and primitive cultural belief systems?' How indeed! The roots are exactly the same.

If we were to travel back through the past in an attempt to trace some of the origins of many of the most powerful and influential forces controlling Rock & Roll today, our journey would take us back down the path of the supernatural. There on that path we would find ourselves staring into the spirit eyes of the HUNGAN (Voodoo priest); unquestionably, one of the ancient forefathers of Rock & Roll.

The power behind the music, the wild dancing it inspires, the hypnotic beat it employs, and most importantly, the source of the inspiration that brought it into existence, are the subjects that must be explored if we are to fully understand this phenomenon called Rock & Roll. Let the expedition begin.

SCREAMIN' JAY HAWKINS

In the early 1950's, a little known blues singer named Jalacey Hawkins recorded a simple blues song which was quite aptly entitled, "I Put A Spell On You". Why would I say *aptly* entitled? It seems that was the Dragon's intention for this song from the beginning; to use it to spellbind the listener. Here is the unusual story of some of the first Voodoo ever heard on American radio.

In its initial form, the slow, blues song 'Spell' became a regional hit which brought Hawkins to the attention of Columbia Records. Because they observed its money making potential, Columbia expressed interest in marketing the song on a wider scale, but unfortunately the original master recording of the song had

Possessed Voodoo man Screamin' Jay Hawkins striking a pose with his cigarette smoking companion skull "Henry."

somehow mysteriously disappeared. Their management department decided they would have Hawkins rerecord it, but this time not as a slow, blues number. They felt, recorded in this way, the song lacked the necessary appeal to market it to a larger audience, so they approached Jay with the request to do a remake of his song in a more up tempo and commercially beneficial rendition. He agreed.

Okeh/Columbia, a subsidiary of the parent company, Columbia Records, sent Jay Hawkins and a team of professional musicians into the recording studio to redo the song. A&R man, Arnold Matson, handled the project.

After trying some different musical approaches it became apparent that nothing was really coming together. Matson, noticing an air of tension in the studio, asked Hawkins what he usually did to loosen up when he was on the road. Hawkins abruptly said, "We party". To Arnold Matson, time was money, so he told Jay that if a party would do the trick, then his company would foot the bill. He sent someone out from the studio to get what he thought would supply a good party -- a few buckets of fried chicken, and a case of cheap wine to wash it down. As soon as the food and drink arrived the party began. Hawkins and the boys not only got loose, they got BLASTED!

After indulging to their fill, Hawkins vaguely remembers, somebody yelled, 'Let's make a record!', and the recording machines were turned on once more. This time Jay Hawkins was to give the recording company a lot more than they originally anticipated. As he began to sing "I Put A Spell On You" again, suddenly some type of presence seemed to seize him. He began grunting, growling, screaming, gurgling in strange unknown languages, and wildly dancing around the studio. He looked more like a Voodoo priest performing a ritual than a blues singer recording a song. No one really knew what was going down, but the stunned and perplexed engineers allowed their machines to continue to run. What they were now capturing on tape was a radically different song than the original one they had heard. It seemed that an uninvited presence of "unknown" origin was apparently in control of Jay Hawkins and the new song.

When he was later asked about his outlandish studio behavior, he had no recollection of the incident whatsoever. Who or what had actually been in control of Hawkins in that recording session? *That is a very good question!*

When Okeh/Columbia, who had financed the project, obtained possession of the studio tapes that had been made that day, they were stunned as well. This was certainly not the same song they had originally heard...of that fact they were sure! What they were listening to now...they weren't so sure. The original blues song had now become so bizarre they didn't know what to do with it, so they decided, rather than scrap it and lose money, they would attempt to recoup some of their investment and release it as a *novelty* record. To everyone's utter amazement it became an instant hit! The voodoo song, "I Put A Spell On You", that had been birthed during that drunken studio session began airing on radio stations all over America, as well as some Canadian stations. Jalacey Hawkins, a relatively unknown blues singer quite suddenly became an overnight sensation. This unearthly song virtually launched his new musical career.

With some prompting from disc jockey Alan Freed (the man most credited for originating the term 'Rock & Roll'), Jay decided to add a new dimension to his act. He adopted the stage name "Screamin' Jay Hawkins", and developed a Voodoo ritual stage production to create the macabre atmosphere needed for showcasing his new hit song using: snakes, Voodoo rattles, a cigarette smoking human skull (named Henry), fire, bells, bones, and a flaming coffin from which he would arise to begin the show. Without a doubt, Voodoo was to be his new theme...just what the Dragon ordered.

Now remember, in the last chapter I mentioned alcohol being an excellent medium for demonic possession? It seems that the devil or devils that had possessed Hawkins in his studio ritual were undoubtedly the same ones prompting the unusual changes in his once tame, by comparison, blues act. Yes, with some invisible spiritual help, Screamin' Jay Hawkins succeeded in transferring his studio voodoo onto vinyl.

Just in case you want to accuse me of fabricating this Hawkins/Voodoo connection, I have recently discovered another very interesting bit of information concerning his family background. It seems that Jay Hawkins was raised by a Blackfoot Indian woman who was somewhat of a voodoo priestess herself. He obviously inherited some of her controlling ancestral spirits (or what is called in Voodoo, the *loa-racine*) along the way. I'll let him explain in his own words what he was actually doing with his music. He told *SPIN* magazine April 1990:

> "If my Blackfoot Indian mother was from Africa you would call her a *witch doctor;* if she was from New Orleans, you'd call her a *voodoo priestess. I JUST PUT IT TO MUSIC."[3]

Now remember, Jay said that, *I didn't.* He was admittedly responsible for putting Voodoo on records all the way back in the *birthing days* of Rock & Roll.

If you really want to know where his music comes from, just look at the back cover of one of his albums entitled, "FRENZY". It says, "Jalacey Hawkins is not an ordinary man and this is not an ordinary record. Play it **AND BE DAMNED.**"; an accurate appraisal to be sure!

Using one of their tools named Screamin' Jay Hawkins, it seemed that the spirits who were responsible for producing the earliest Rock & Roll were no longer attempting to keep a low profile. They were aggressively emerging from their initial obscurity and beginning to make themselves clearly known. Satan was now putting his cloven hoof in the Rock & Roll door for the purpose it had actually been created...to spread *DARKNESS* to the people.

BO DIDDLEY

Another early American Rock & Roll pioneer to effectively use a hypnotic voodoo beat as the focal point of his music was Ellas McDaniel, or as he was better known on the streets of Chicago, Bo Diddley.

Just like Jay Hawkins, he also began his recording career with Okeh Records; but soon transferred to a Chess Records subsidiary label called Checker. One of the first songs he recorded for the label was a song entitled, "I'm A Man", which according to Rolling Stone History of Rock & Roll was "...loaded with sexual braggadocio and seething with menace."

But for this book our interest lies mainly in another one of his hit songs entitled, "Who Do You Love". This song also seems to be "seething with menace", but in a different way. Here are some of the lyrics to the song:

> "I walk 47 miles of barbed wire
> I wear a cobra snake for a necktie
> I got a brand new house on the roadside
> Made from rattlesnake hide
> I got a brand new chimney made on top
> Made out of a HUMAN SKULL
> Now come on and take a little walk with me Arlene
> And tell me who do you love"

Now let's examine for just a moment a possible origin for these rather bizarre song lyrics. If we look beneath the surface, we might find an unexpected source for the lyrical content of this early Rock & Roll classic -- the Hindu gods of India. I will explain.

SHIVA THE DESTROYER

The predominant religion of India is Hinduism of which there are many variations. Hindus can worship any number of a multitude of deities; from the monkey god, HANUMAN, to the god of thunder and rain, INDRA, to their

Above: The Hindu god Shiva with his wife or consort Parvati. Notice the cobra snake around the neck.

Below: Hindu deity Shiva fighting a demon opponent. Notice the cobra snake around the neck. Also notice the demon king using the black magic hexagram or 6 pointed star on a pole to defend himself.

concept of the Supreme God they call KRISHNA. There are literally hundreds of thousands of gods and goddesses from which to choose.

The Hindu concept of the Christian Trinity or triune Godhead consists of, not the Father, the Son, and the Holy Spirit; but the gods BRAHMA the creator, VISHNU the preserver, and SHIVA the *DESTROYER*.

Now why have I suddenly shifted my attention from Bo Diddley to Hinduism? Very simple. Look at the lyrics to the song "Who Do You Love" and you can definitely make a strong connection between the two. One line in particular makes this connection evident. The line I'm referring to is the one that says, "I wear a COBRA SNAKE FOR A NECKTIE". I know that this may seem to be a rather strange song lyric until you find out what it actually represents.

If you were to see a depiction of the Hindu god SHIVA the destroyer, your attention would immediately be drawn to one aspect of his unusual image. There is a COBRA SNAKE *AROUND HIS NECK*. The Hindu god SHIVA is literally wearing, as Bo Diddley's song says, *"a cobra snake for a necktie"*.

This unexpected marriage of Rock & Roll and Hinduism dominates most of this song. Bo Diddley also sings these moribund lyrics:

> "I have a TOMBSTONE HAND and a GRAVEYARD MIND
> I'm just 22 and I DON'T MIND DYIN'"

Now let's examine the basic theme of this song. Many words associated with death are used: SKULL, TOMBSTONE, GRAVEYARD, and DYIN'. Here, in one of the earliest Rock & Roll songs ever recorded (1956), we find lyrical imagery that can be traced to the mystical "spiritual" practices of the YOGIS. Religions researcher, Mircea Eliade, once again explains. He writes:

> "On the level of highest Indian spirituality, the *CEMETERY, CORPSES, SKELETONS,* were revalorized and incorporated into an ascetico-mystical symbolism; to *MEDITATE SEATED ON A CORPSE,* to wear a SKULL, etc., now represented *SPIRITUAL* exercises..."[4]

Interestingly enough, however, it is not only the yogis who behave in this manner. The Hindu god Shiva, whom they worship, has also been known to

Shiva the Destroyer (cobra snake around his neck) with Parvati stringing severed heads onto a necklace. Notice symbols of death at bottom of picture.

manifest similar necrophilic behavior. According to the book <u>Indian Mythology</u>, among his other depictions Shiva is also represented as:

> "...haunting cemeteries...looking like a madman, with no clothes, smeared with ashes, with matted hair, and with *SKULLS* and *HUMAN BONES* about his person."[5]

In all the documentaries I have watched dealing with the subject of Hinduism, I have seen many of the yogis appearing in exactly the same manner. So as you can clearly see by these examples, not only do the yogis, as well as their "highest" gods, seem to revel in images connected with death, rather than being repulsed by them; but this grotesque imagery also directly correlates with the lyrics to the aforementioned Bo Diddley song.

This affinity towards death is not shared by all spiritual belief systems. Christianity in particular sees death as a temporarily unavoidable tragedy that has been manifested on the earth as a direct result of SIN.

God told Adam in the Garden of Eden that the day he would eat of a specific fruit, the one from the tree of the knowledge of good and evil, he would DIE. He disobeyed God, ate the forbidden fruit...and he died; which very simply meant, at that moment, he became spiritually separated from the HOLY GOD and Creator who was his first Father. The sin of Adam became the doorway which also allowed physical death to enter into this world system.

The Bible details another incident which deals with death when Jesus Christ encountered a man who was living among the TOMBS OF THE DEAD. It says:

> *"And they came over unto the other side of the sea, into the country of the Gadarenes. And when he [Jesus] was come out of the ship, immediately there met him out of the TOMBS a man with an* **UNCLEAN SPIRIT**, *who had his dwelling* **among the TOMBS.**"

> Mark 5:1-3

Now, even though the yogis view this same activity of dwelling among the tombs of the DEAD as being a *highly spiritual* practice, it is clear that the Bible has just given us the true reason why the Gadarene demoniac (the title by which this historical figure is known) was living *among the tombs*. In reality, his level of spirituality was anything *but* high. His thanatologic behavior was a direct result of DEMONIC POSSESSION! Do you suppose in the yogis' case it's any different? I can assure you, it is NOT.

Bo Diddley's early Rock & Roll classic, "Who Do You Love", was without a doubt, written under the influence of the same spirits or gods of darkness that have courted the Hindu yogis for thousands of years.

When yogis die the demonic spirits which inhabit them don't die along with their host bodies. They simply move on *into NEW ONES!* And living in India is not a prerequisite for possession.

It is another intriguing fact that just a few years ago one of Bo Diddley's biggest fans and emulators reintroduced this same song to a whole new generation of Rock & Roll children. The man who rerecorded the song was George Thorogood.

What's really interesting to me, however, is the name of his band...THE *DESTROYERS*. Now remember the name of the Hindu god you just read about a few moments ago? His name was SHIVA...*THE DESTROYER!* George

Thorogood and *The Destroyers* -- SHIVA *the DESTROYER*. Hmmmm...fasci-
nating correlation, wouldn't you say?

Okay, right about now you might be saying, 'This is all very interesting, but
a few people being involved in something doesn't necessarily make a good case
against it'; and of course, you are right. But I have not finished tracking the
Voodoo trail through Rock & Roll just yet. We will now continue our search
by delving into the unusual life of one of the most influential Rock & Roll
musicians of our time: a "Voodoo Child" named Jimi.

VOODOO CHILD (Slight Return)

Aquarian voodoo child guitarist Jimi Hendrix during the sacrificial burning of his guitar at Monterey Pop Festival; his first major American appearance.

Jimi Hendrix was considered to be a true innovator of the heavy, acid, blues/rock sounds of the late 1960's and early 70's. However, what Hendrix was actually doing with his music was, in essence, not new at all. It seems that he was just an electric *hungan* who, with a Fender guitar and a Marshall stack, decided to add a little volume to his Voodoo.

We started this chapter with a few lines from a Jimi Hendrix song called "Voodoo Child". It appears that after a closer look at the life of Jimi Hendrix, the words to his song, "Voodoo Child", which he recorded on his "Electric Ladyland" album, were more autobiographical than even *he* might have suspected.

In the Jimi Hendrix biography entitled, 'Scuse Me While I Kiss the Sky, is a very revealing account of an incident that took place between Jimi and one of the musicians with whom he frequently jammed. It is the remembrance of a conversation Hendrix once had with a conga drummer who called himself Rocki. His real name was Kwasi Dzidzornu, but for this account, we will call him Rocki as well.

The most interesting piece of information I discovered about Rocki was his family background. It seems that Rocki's father was a *VOODOO PRIEST* and Rocki knew quite a bit about Voodoo himself. Here is the Rocki and Hendrix encounter excerpted from the book:

"Jimi and Rocki first played together at the Speakeasy...that was how they met and became friends.

Rocki's father was a Voodoo priest and the chief drummer of a village in Ghana, West Africa...one of the first things that Rocki asked Jimi was where he got that voodoo rhythm from. When Jimi demurred, Rocki went on to explain in his halting English that many of the signature rhythms that Jimi played were very often the *same* rhythms that his father played in voodoo ceremonies. The way Jimi danced to the rhythms of his playing reminded Rocki of the ceremonial dances to the rhythms his father played to the god Oxun, the god of thunder and lightning. The ceremony is called voodoshi. As a child in the village, Rocki would carve wooden representations of the gods. They also represented his ancestors. These were the gods they worshiped.

They would jam a lot in Jimi's house. One time they were jamming and Jimi stopped and asked Rocki pointblank, 'You communicate with God, do you?' Rocki said, 'Yes, I communicate with God.'"[6]

That may have been what Rocki thought, but I can assure you he was *WRONG*. God takes no part whatsoever in voodoo ceremonies. Rocki did communicate with someone or something, but IT *WASN'T GOD*.

Jimi, according to this son of a voodoo priest, was also using Voodoo. This voodoo revelation concerning the life of Jimi Hendrix, however, is just the tip of the iceberg.

Jimi considered his music to be more than just a collection of interesting and imaginative songs. To him, it was spiritual worship; a tool he used to preach a message to his followers. He explained this to *Life* magazine the year before he died. He said:

"...music is a spiritual thing of its own. You can hypnotize people with music, and when you get them at their weakest point you can preach into their subconscious whatever you want to say."[7]

The doctrine that Hendrix preached was an occult one to be sure. Jimi was a serious believer in reincarnation, astral projection, witchcraft, and even DEMONIC POSSESSION, often speaking very candidly, as well as writing songs about these mystical subjects.

On the subject of witchcraft, Hendrix said:

"Things like *witchcraft*, which is a form of exploration and imagination, have been banned by the establishment and called evil. It's because people are frightened to find out the full power of the mind..."[8]

Jimi Hendrix, just as the yogis, shamans, voodoo priests, and sorcerers do, often used perception altering drugs to unlock this "full power of the mind". LSD, THC, hashish, and even STP, a very powerful hallucinogen, were some of his favorites. The title of one song he wrote called, "Stars That Play with Laughing Sam's Dice", is actually an acronym dedicated to the drugs STP and LSD (the title of Beatles song, "Lucy in the Sky with Diamonds", served the same purpose). He was using these drugs to aid him in his search for "spiritual" awakening, but what he acquired as a result of that search is even more interesting.

On the soundtrack album from the movie based on the life of Jimi Hendrix is the sad evidence of his spiritual dilemma. The last interview section on Side 4 tells the tragic story. His friend and producer Alan Douglas explains:

"Now one of the biggest things about Jimi was what he believed, and he believed that he was *POSSESSED* by some spirit, and I got to believe it myself; and that's what we had to deal with all the time -- He really believed it and was wrestling with it constantly."[9]

Was Douglas the only one privy to Jimi's spiritual *possession* dilemma? No he wasn't. One of Hendrix's girlfriends, Fayne Pridgon, was also aware of his problem. She said:

"He used to talk about some devil or something was *IN* him. He didn't know what made him act the way he acted and what made him say the things he said, and the songs and different things like that...just come out of him...It seems to me he was so tormented and just torn apart and like he really was obsessed, you know, with something really evil...He said, 'You're from Georgia...you should know how people drive demons out' -- He used to talk about us going...and having some root lady or somebody see if she could *drive this demon out of him.*"[10]

FAYNE PRIDGON

Jimi Hendrix, just like many of the other Rock & Roll innovators of history, *knew* that another spirit was in control of his life.

As I continued my research into the life of Hendrix, more and more telltale evidence of demonic possession began to surface. I saw how, through the use of drugs and experimenting with the occult, he had actually lost control of his will. Often I would read where he would suddenly, without explanation, fly into fits of rage, resulting in quite regrettable behavior for which he would later be forced to apologize. One incident in particular reveals what I mean.

In his book on Hendrix, David Henderson gives this account:

"Vishwa [a friend of Jimi's] heard screams coming from the bedroom, he ran in: Jimi had the beautiful Eurasian girl, Meryl, down on the floor and was BEATING HER HEAD AGAINST IT."[11]

You might find it interesting to note that black tantric Hindu sorcery, Voodoo, Shamanism, Satanism, and many thoroughly documented cases of true demonic possession all have one particular manifestation in common: VIOLENCE! Was Jimi Hendrix any different? Regretfully, he was not. It is painfully clear, what not only motivated, but also controlled guitar hero Jimi Hendrix. The voodoo, occult, Hindu, drug connection was once again emanating from the same spirit source.

Though I am spending these pages exposing these pathetic, Dragon-manipulated people, it fills me with a deep sadness to discover how Satan literally destroys them one by one.

At one point in my life, Jimi Hendrix was one of my biggest idols...but not anymore. We will not be sharing an eternal life of peace on some distant astral shore as I once anticipated. He followed the dark path...I came to the LIGHT.

Jimi Hendrix believed in reincarnation. On September 18, 1970, in the early morning hours of the day, he died...and found out he was *WRONG*. He was not floating around on some astral plane waiting to be born again into any new lives; the only one he had been gifted with was now eternally lost.

On February 6, 1983, also in the early morning hours of the day, about 2:30 a.m. to be precise, I found out that my belief in reincarnation was wrong as well. But I found out something that Jimi never did discover until it was too late. I could be BORN AGAIN without ever having to die. Yes, in a pastor's office in Detroit, Michigan, with a God-loving and God-fearing evangelist named Michael Mills, I prayed to receive Jesus Christ as my Lord and Savior. That was the day THE LIGHTS WENT *ON*. I had spent my whole life looking for the truth. Little did I know that Jesus, who *IS* the TRUTH, had been patiently waiting for me to find Him. That night He came to me and I surrendered my will to Him and accepted His forgiveness for all my sins. I became alive in the SPIRIT for the very first time. Jesus rescued me that night from the damnation of the Dragon right then and there.

Jimi Hendrix was involved in electronic voodoo and he knew it. He was tortured, trapped, and constantly tormented by the evil spirits he had summoned through his drug use and his music. He eventually discovered his inability to escape them by his own power, but he never turned to Jesus for release. He paid for this tragic mistake with the ultimate price...his eternal life.

There are other groups who are also heavily involved in the occult religion of Voodoo. Two of those groups are two of the most well known and popular bands in the world today: The Rolling Stones and the Talking Heads. We will discuss the Stones at later time; but for now , the Talking Heads.

DAVID BYRNE

The lead vocalist, guitarist, and main spokesman for the group Talking Heads is presently very involved in the voodoo spirit religion of Brazil called Candom-

Talking Heads leader David Byrne posing in Brazil with Candomble priest friend, Balbino Daniel de Paula.

blé. His name is David Byrne. Not only does Byrne have voodoo flags used in worship of the Candomblé voodoo gods hanging in his apartment, a testimony to his support of Candomblé, but he decided to share this occult pagan religion with the entire country.

On June 5, 1989, PBS television aired a special program called Ilé Aiyé (which is translated 'House of life'). It was a documentary directed by David Byrne which showed the people of Bahia, Brazil celebrating their religion of Candomblé. Certain footage in Byrne's film took the viewer behind the scenes of a Candomblé spirit possession ritual while it was in progress. The audience was able to watch the priests and priestesses of this South American religion as they allowed themselves to become demon possessed.

The Candomblé "clergy" act as mediums who draw the Yoruba "gods" they serve *into their bodies* through their dances of invocation and worship. Once they become possessed, the individual spirits within them receive sacrificial offerings, answer questions, and perform healings.

Contrary to the belief system of the Candomblé religion, these spirits are not gods and goddesses concerned for the well being of their "flock". The Bible reveals their true identity. It identifies them as devils who work miracles (Rev. 16:14).

Through his own personal involvement, Byrne is actively promoting the religion of Candomblé.

Does David Byrne, one of the Dragon's newest promoters, recognize any similarity between Rock & Roll and these Candomblé possession ceremonies he has witnessed? As a matter of fact, he does. In an interview concerning his involvement with Candomblé, featured in a recent issue of *Rolling Stone* magazine, Byrne explains the remarkable similarity he has discovered between Rock & Roll and the pagan religion he has embraced. He says:

> "If you go back in the history of American popular music, you're constantly finding elements of Yoruba influence. The *rhythms* are there, the sensibility in the *lyrics* is there too. Even **Little Richard**. If you grow up with that, you've already got a taste of it. So when you see Candomblé, you say to yourself, 'hey, **this is part of where it all comes from**. It's *NOT* SOMETHING EXOTIC."[12]

In the same *Rolling Stone* magazine article, the Yale professor who interviewed Byrne wrote these words evaluating the aforementioned PBS special:

> "The gods descend-but-little is overtly explained to the viewer, who is free to wonder at the gods' sacred visages, their color-coded attributes. Toward the end of the film, the camera lingers on the faces of these gods. Face after face. Object after object. In the background music is played on a BERIMBAU, a bowed instrument that in ancient Africa was used to put people in a *MEDITA-TIVE STATE*. And that's what Byrne's film does all the way."[13]
>
> ROBERT FARRIS THOMPSON
> PROFESSOR OF AFRICAN-AMERICAN ART HISTORY
> YALE UNIVERSITY

This Yale college professor has rightly observed and commented on the fact that Byrne's film on Candomblé was being used to put the viewer in a meditative **state.** (There's that word again!)

Through his own personal beliefs, his television special, and a few recent albums promoting their music, David Byrne, being assisted by the spirits who created this South American voodoo religion, has allowed the influence of Candomblé to flow unobstructed into the souls of the American people. And if you think that David Byrne (who, by the way, won an academy award for the musical score he wrote for the movie, "The Last Emperor") has no influence on the culture that we live in, THINK AGAIN!

Voodoo warrior David Byrne and his group The Talking Heads have proven to be one more popular weapon in the Dragon's arsenal.

But remember what Byrne said earlier about the Voodoo roots of Little Richard's music? Well, Little Richard just so happens to *agree!* His comment about his own understanding of the Rock & Roll/Voodoo connection:

> "My own belief about Rock 'n' Roll -- and there have been a lot of phrases attributed to me over the years -- is this: I believe this kind of music is DEMONIC. I have seen the rock groups and the punk-rock people in this country. And some of their lyrics is demonic. *They talk against God.* A lot of the beats in music today are taken from **VOODOO**, from the voodoo drums. If you study music in rhythms, like I have, you'll see that is true."[14]

As you can clearly see, Little Richard *KNEW* (as David Byrne also recognized) he had been using Voodoo years before in the earliest Rock & Roll! Voodoo and the earliest Rock & Roll the same?? YES. Surprised again? We're only just beginning.

Heartbeat of the Dragon

CHAPTER 5

MAD GODS AND ENGLISHMEN

While all the demon-inspired music of Little Richard, Jerry Lee Lewis, Bo Diddley, and Screamin' Jay Hawkins, to name but a few, was being foisted upon the unsuspecting American people, the occult Rock & Roll lion of Britain was also beginning to roar.

Through the late 1800's on into the 1900's, many British based, occult organizations were formed. The Theosophical Society, The Hermetic Order of The Golden Dawn, The Order of The Silver Star, Freemasonry, and Rosicrucianism were but a few of the many esoteric societies that found their homes in England.

Even though Britain had previously outlawed witchcraft and her society placed a stigma on the practitioners of many of the other occult "arts", by the 1950's witchcraft and spiritism were being practiced openly and without penalty. With all this occultism already firmly in place, would the Rock & Roll Dragon be far behind? As you could have guessed...not likely. The early 1960's witnessed England suddenly filled with people who were caught up in the occult; and British Rock & Roll was about to follow suit.

JACK THE RIFFER

In the 1960's, a young man named Lord David Sutch decided to bring a vaudevillian influence to British Rock & Roll. He received much of his musical inspiration from people such as Little Richard, Chuck Berry, Jerry Lee Lewis, and Screamin' Jay Hawkins.

He loved early American Rock & Roll and adopted the late 1950's style as his own, often delighting his audiences with classics such as: "Good Golly Miss Molly", "Johnny B. Goode", "Long Tall Sally", and "Great Balls of Fire".

Although he was partial to straight ahead Rock & Roll music, he especially liked the strange voodoo theatrics of Screamin' Jay Hawkins. This inspired him to assume the stage name Screaming Lord Sutch, and add a variety of horror show props to his Rock & Roll stage production.

One reporter wrote of witnessing a concert starring Screaming Lord Sutch and the Savages:

> "It was dark and a chilly wind blew. The crowd stirred as the Rock 'n' Roll All Stars struck up the death march and howled ghoulishly into their microphones.
>
> Suddenly a green light appeared in the distance and down the hillside came a procession of hooded monks, bearing a black coffin, lit by two flaming torches.
>
> Excitement rose as the pall-bearers made their way among the crowd and the music came to a climax as the coffin was put on the stage. Three spine chilling screams emitted from within, and in true Sutch style, a headless, bloody, body with grotesque hands emerged.
>
> So Screaming Lord Sutch, David to his friends, started his show on Friday, at the Carshalton Park Rock 'n' Roll Festival."[1]

His passion for shocking horror show theatrics prompted him to write his own Rock & Roll songs with titles such as, "Hands of Jack the Ripper", a song written about the murderous madman called Jack the Ripper, who many years before had stalked, murdered, and dismembered a number of London prostitutes, quietly and efficiently carving them up with a scalpel. Because of his affinity for the grotesque and the macabre many people even called Lord Sutch the new Jack the Ripper of Rock & Roll.

Just as his namesake Screamin' Jay Hawkins had done, Screaming Lord Sutch also incorporated a coffin into his act. But where Screamin' Jay Hawkins chose Voodoo as his vehicle for drawing attention, Screaming Lord Sutch opted for a more tantric approach, using bloody headless corpses and mock murders.

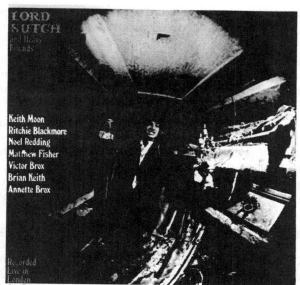

Hands of Jack the Ripper album cover, Screaming Lord Sutch standing in a coffin with knife in hand.

You will find it interesting to note that lying in a coffin is a major part of the black Tantra rites of Hinduism; where a yogi will actually sleep inside an exhumed coffin with the decayed remains of a dead body as an act of "purification". Now as gruesome as this may seem, this behavior is rather mild considering the numerous other abominable practices in which they joyfully partake on their journey to attaining "spiritual *wholeness*". In his book, <u>Riders of the Cosmic Circuit</u>, author Tal Brooke explains:

> "The TANTRICS had it down. Surrender by degradation -- *EAT-ING FECES, coitus* [sexual intercourse] with the *DEAD, CAN-NIBALISM, HUMAN SACRIFICE* -- remember 'blowing the lid off conventional morality' -- *orgies*, worship of SHIVA...Siva...Satan, The Ancient One."[2]

Now, I know you might be saying that all the blood, murder, and mayhem of Screaming Lord Sutch was just show business fantasy, but I would quickly remind you that it is a matter of record that repetitious vicarious participation in fantasy, especially EVIL fantasy, often gives way to actual participation in evil reality.

Screaming Lord Sutch not only assaulted his audiences with images of murder, mayhem, and occultism, but he also injected this tantric madness into the souls of the young and impressionable musicians who played in his back-up group.

Many who would go on to become superstars, at one time or another, played with this "Jack the Ripper" of early British Rock & Roll. Among those he influenced: Jeff Beck, Keith Moon, Nicky Hopkins, Jimmy Page, Matthew Fisher, John Bonham, Rick Nielsen, Noel Redding, Nicky Simper, and Ritchie Blackmore. Some of these same musicians, who played in his backup group called The Savages, later became *true* followers of the dark path of the occult.

Once again, you can clearly see the Dragon's minions were manipulating musicians such as Screaming Lord Sutch and his friends in an attempt to bring the dark occult side of Indian mysticism into the mainstream of British Rock & Roll. Implementation of the latter day plan of destruction that had previously hatched in the Evil One's mind was obviously now fully under way.

GRAHAM BOND

Another soldier of the Evil One was a man named Graham Bond. Many people consider him to be the father of British rhythm and blues. Bond played with, as well as inaugurated, many of the future blues and rock stars of England during the time of his recording career, including: John McLaughlin, of Mahavishnu Orchestra fame; Ginger Baker and Jack Bruce of the late 60's supergroup power trio called the Cream; and Rick Grech, who joined Eric Clapton, Ginger Baker, and Steve Winwood to form Blind Faith.

Now you might ask why I would call Graham Bond a soldier of the Evil One? Very Simple. He and his wife were totally obsessed with the occult, especially ceremonial magic. This interest revolved particularly around the teachings of a black magician of the early 1900's by the name of Aleister Crowley. Bond even believed himself to be the actual son of the infamous diabolist. (More on Crowley later.)

Front cover of Graham Bond album dedicated to Aleister Crowley: Holy Magick. Note the use of the "K" in the word magick. Something originated by Crowley and a telltale sign of a true devotee.

After his original band, the Graham Bond Organisation, broke up in 1968, he married a British singer named Diane Stewart and they both delved full-force into a study of the occult. Together they formed a new music group called Holy Magick (Magick [with a 'k'] being the name Crowley gave to his own brand of sorcery), which was dedicated to Crowley and his teachings; but soon both the band and the marriage failed.

Bond tried to start another group in 1973 called Magus (the name given to a high level sorcerer) but it failed as well. Not long after that, at the young age of 37...he was dead.

To this day his death is an unsolved mystery. On May 8, 1974, just a few months after he was released from a mental hospital, his body was discovered under the wheels of a stationary tube train at Finsbury Park Station in London, England. No one, it seems, knows what actually happened to cause his death, and those who do have any ideas aren't saying much. However, I did discover a rather interesting piece of information from the owner of a record store where

Graham Bond Organisation - Bond, far right, with Jack Bruce, second from the right, and Ginger Baker, second from the left, who would become 2/3's of the super group "Cream".

I sometimes buy my research material. He told me that Bond's death is believed by some who knew him well to have been the result of a curse which was placed on him by a black magician and follower of Aleister Crowley named Kenneth Anger. With what I know of Anger, Crowley, his followers, and their curses, this doesn't surprise me in the least.

Many of the musicians Graham Bond worked with were deeply influenced by his magickal (spelled with a 'k' in true Crowley fashion) lifestyle which included heavy drug involvement. Though the Dragon had used up and then quickly discarded this man, by the time of his demise, his occult influence had already been embedded into the souls of some of the most famous Rock & Roll musicians of this age.

The black magick, drug life of Graham Bond and the black tantric horror show theatrics of Screaming Lord Sutch had a direct influence on some of the most famous groups in the history of Rock & Roll. Groups such as: THE WHO, CHEAP TRICK, RAINBOW, DEEP PURPLE, THE MAHAVISHNU OR-

CHESTRA, THE CREAM, LED ZEPPELIN, PROCOL HARUM, BLIND FAITH, THE JEFF BECK GROUP, THE YARDBIRDS, and THE JIMI HENDRIX EXPERIENCE, not to mention three cast members from the satanically inspired rock opera JESUS CHRIST SUPERSTAR. (Two of these cast members, Victor & Annette Brox, sang with *both* Graham Bond *and* Screaming Lord Sutch.)

This occult/Rock & Roll union with some of the most popular, innovative, and trend setting bands of our era was a major accomplishment in the Dragon's grand design. The time had come to energize his new flock. But why do it then, and why use Rock & Roll? The answer is obvious. If he would have openly attempted to promote Shamanism, Voodoo, Tantric Hinduism, or Satanism as a catalyst for spirit possession and control to the modern twentieth century cultures of England and America in the 1960's and 70's, these pagan practices would have quickly been rejected. But...if he were to subtly present these same occult religious ideas using a more deceptive vehicle like Rock & Roll, by the time anyone caught on to his scheme, it would already be too late to stop it. The indoctrination of an entire generation would have already been completed. That was the plan and that is *exactly what he did*.

On the surface, Rock & Roll appeared to be relatively harmless; but underneath that thin veneer of "fun" the Dragon was fully aware of its devastating capabilities. It was specifically designed to instigate REBELLION in the listener (the Bible equates rebellion to the "...*sin of witchcraft*" -- see I SAM. 15:23), as well as undermining their inborn God-ordained moral code. Through the overpowering musical force of Rock & Roll, Satan knew he could weaken souls and ultimately bring about their total possession. He would use these blind, but willing, pawns to accomplish his final goal...they would be used to assist him in ushering in the DOMINION OF THE BEAST (see Ch. 1).

THE RESTRAINING FACTOR

The only real obstacles in the Dragon's path preventing him from setting up *his* kingdom on Earth, the kingdom of the anti- Christ, are Jesus Christ and his Church. His hatred for them both is no secret.

On the cover of one of the issues of The Cloven Hoof, the membership literature distributed by the Church of Satan, is a picture of a dragon devouring the body of a crucified, dead Jesus Christ directly from the cross. Satan, the Dragon, this church's master, has made it his life's ambition to promote a dead and powerless Jesus and devour true Christianity.

Let me give you a few examples of what I mean. Here are a couple of "scriptures" from the Satanic Bible:

"I dip my forefinger in the watery blood of your **impotent mad redeemer**, and write over his thorn torn brow the TRUE **prince of evil the king of slaves.**"[3]

Book of Satan 1:6

And again it says:

"I gaze into the glassy eye of your fearsome Jehovah, and **pluck him by the beard**; I uplift a broad-axe, and split open his worm-eaten skull!"[4]

Book of Satan 1:10

The final example I will give shows the venomous contempt Satan has for the cross of Christ as he spews forth these words through his unwitting medium Anton Szandor LaVey:

"Behold the **crucifix**; what does it symbolize? **pallid incompetence hanging on a tree.**"[5]

Book of Satan 2:1

Though the creation of the crucifix was never God's desire in the first place (see Ex. 20:4,5 where God commanded to make *NO* images of himself), it is clear by that last satanic scripture that *Satan loves to represent a **DEAD** Christ.* He is not afraid to mock this icon that depicts Jesus *still ON* the cross. This mockery of the crucifix is clearly shown on many album covers and is also expressed by many Rock & Roll musicians and singers who adorn themselves with this symbol (Madonna being the most infamous). What Satan *is* afraid of, however, is the fact that Jesus was taken *OFF* that cross, put into a tomb, and ROSE AGAIN FROM THE DEAD three days later. He is no longer dead or on that cross. Why continue to falsely depict Him that way? Ask Satan, the creation of the crucifix was *HIS* idea...not God's.

Well, anyway, you can clearly see by those last three examples of satanic "scriptures" that they truly come straight from the heart of the Dragon, the **FATHER** OF ROCK & ROLL.

With the occult/drug connection firmly locked in place in both England and America in the 1950's and early 1960's, by the middle 1960's, the Devil was prepared to go in for the kill. Since Jesus and Christianity were keeping his new "Christ" and his NEW DARK AGE at bay, he needed to find a more potent vehicle to implement his REAL agenda. Besides possessing the young, it was imperative for the Dragon to remove any rational concept whatsoever of a personal Savior and a Holy and loving God from the hearts and minds of a whole generation. He was to find the vehicle which would accomplish this task in his best modern day musical weapon yet...The Beatles.

Heartbeat of the Dragon

CHAPTER 6

MAGICAL MISERY TOUR

"They were like *mediums.* They weren't conscious of all they were saying, but it was **coming through them.**"[1]

YOKO ONO LENNON

"When the real music comes to me--the music of the spheres, the music that surpasseth understanding--that has nothing to do with me, 'cause I'm just the *channel.* The only joy for me is for it to be given to me, and to transcribe it like a *medium*...those moments are what I live for.[2]

JOHN LENNON

As you just read in the words of John Lennon and Yoko Ono, the Beatles truly *were* **mediums** being used for a specific purpose. Unquestionably, I could write an entire volume dealing with many different aspects of their great spiritual contribution to the Dragon's plan; but for this book I will only zero in on two principal areas of concern:

#1. Their hatred for God, the Holy Bible, Jesus Christ, and Christianity.

#2. Their unabashed promotion of eastern mysticism, drugs, and the occult.

IN THE BEGINNING - THE FAB FOUR

On the night of February 9, 1964, if a person would have tuned-in to the most popular Sunday night television show in America, as most of the country did on that night, they would have seen four clean-cut looking British boys playing their energetic Rock & Roll for the screaming and hysterical studio audience. The song that was virtually being drowned out by the constant screams of this overtly exuberant audience was entitled, "I Want To Hold You Hand". Ed Sullivan had just introduced America to...The Beatles.

Within the next few years they portrayed themselves to the public as quick-witted, zany characters who just liked to play Rock & Roll music and have fun. Beatle movies like "A Hard Days Night", released in July of 1964, greatly enhanced their innocent, fun-loving image. This image, however, was a big part of the plan that had been coordinated in the minds of those who were promoting the "Fab Four". Their clean-cut image was carefully orchestrated to give them a wider public acceptance than they would have received had they continued to wear the black leather jackets and worn blue jeans which had previously been their basic stage attire.

The truth is that while their outward image might have been altered to fool the public by outfitting them with neatly trimmed hairstyles and well tailored matching suits, their wild, debauched lifestyles remained unchanged. Let's just say the old cliché, "sex, drugs, and rock & roll", would not have been wasted on John, Paul, George, and Ringo. They lived on a rather steady diet of drink, drugs, and *dainties,* if you get my drift.

But that wasn't the Dragon's grand design for The Beatles anyway. They weren't supposed to be the champions of a party lifestyle; there were plenty of other bands, such as the Rolling Stones, that could fill that niche. Instead, he raised them up to be the youngest and most influential *anti-christs* the modern world has ever known.

With a little help from their friends, the media (also predominantly owned and operated by the Dragon), it didn't take long for their fans to understand and identify the mindset of their mission. Their hatred for Christianity was something they made no attempt to conceal. They also took turns taking potshots at Jesus.

John Lennon incurred the wrath of Christians everywhere in the summer of 1966 when he made the now infamous statement to a reporter for the *Evening Standard* after reading a very popular diatribe against Christianity called The Passover Plot. He said:

> "Christianity will go, it will vanish and shrink. I needn't argue about that. I'm right and will be proved right. Jesus was all right, but his disciples were thick and ordinary. It's them twisting it that ruins it for me. **We're more popular than JESUS now.**"[3]

Atheist, Paul McCartney agreed when he proclaimed:

> "We probably seem to be anti-religious...**none of us BELIEVES IN GOD.**"[4]

George Harrison, who readily adopted a belief in eastern mysticism, said:

> "There is much more validity to **Hinduism than anything in Christianity.**"[5]

Ringo Starr echoed the sentiments of Lennon and McCartney saying:

> "We're not anti-Christ...just anti-Christian. **JESUS IS DEAD.**"[6]

Even their press officer Derek Taylor was a witness to their hatred for Christianity when he said:

> "I'm anti-Christ...but **they're so anti-Christ they shock** *ME* which isn't an easy thing to do."[7]

Yes, it seems those lovable little "mop tops" were very, very anti-Christ...but why? When their innovative smash hit album, "Sgt. Peppers Lonely Hearts Club Band", made its debut, a possible clue to the anti-Christ attitude of the Beatles may have been revealed.

When Ringo Starr was asked in an interview, why the people pictured on the cover of "Sgt. Pepper" were chosen, he said:

> "We just thought we would like to put together a lot of people we like and admire."[8]

Paul McCartney, in an interview with *Musician* magazine, also spoke about choosing those who would grace the "Sgt. Pepper" album cover. He remembers:

Above: Front cover of "Sgt. Pepper" Top Row: second from the left Aleister Crowley, 7th from right Carl Jung. Second Row Down: Second from right Paramahansa Yogananda , 4th from right Karl Marx, third from right H.G. Wells
Below: Close up of Crowley from Beatle album

"And we were going to have photos on the wall of all our heroes: Marlon Brando in his leather jacket, Einstein -- it could be anybody who **we'd ever thought was *good*.** Cult heroes."[9]

Some of those people they chose to admire which appear on the cover are also some of the most anti-Christian figures in history. Among the "good" people occupying this position of admiration: God-hater and one of the fathers of communism--Karl Marx; occultist/psychologist--Carl Jung; irreverent radical comedian--Lenny Bruce; Hindu guru--Sri Paramahansa Yogananda, as well as three other well known gurus; and New Age/occult author--H.G. Wells. With "good" influences like these it isn't very difficult to imagine how a prevailing anti-Christ attitude could develop in the minds of the Beatles.

However, the person in the top row, second from the left, is of greater concern to me than the rest; for without a doubt he was as anti-Christ as anyone could ever be. Who is this bald- headed and rather sullen looking character? He is occult black magician, Aleister Crowley.

To my knowledge, the Beatles have never really elaborated on their connection with Crowley, but a close examination of his teachings and their professed beliefs show some definite parallels.

Aleister Crowley was deeply involved in the occult as was Beatle John Lennon. Numerology and the Tarot were favorites of them both.

Much of what Crowley believed and taught was based on tantric Hinduism. All of the Beatles at one time or another experimented with aspects of this eastern religious philosophy. Lennon, at one time, was so deeply involved in Transcendental Meditation (a different name for the same yogic discipline of tantric Hinduism as taught by Maharishi Mahesh Yogi) that it noticeably altered his personality. John Lennon eventually renounced TM but by then much of the spiritual damage to his steadily decaying soul had already been done. Two of the other Beatles, Paul McCartney and Ringo Starr, after their brief infatuation with the Maharishi also renounced TM (though Ringo and Hinduism have remained friends).

George Harrison, on the other hand, wholeheartedly accepted and adopted Hinduism as his own. Over the years, it was reflected in his music with songs such as, "Within You Without You" on the Beatles "Sgt. Pepper" album; "Life Itself" on his solo album "Somewhere In England; and the smash hit song "My

Sweet Lord" from his three record set tribute to Hinduism called "All Things Must Pass".

More importantly, however, than his tantric Hindu leanings was Crowley's utter loathing of Christianity which he expressed most vividly in his writings. Could these writings have effected the fervent anti-Christ attitude of the Beatles? That is a distinct possibility.

Another important determining factor in developing an anti- Christian attitude, such as the one consistently demonstrated by the Beatles, can also be traced to their extensive use of drugs, especially that of LSD.

What is this strange drug and what does it actually do? If you want the answer, read on. You might get more than you expected.

CHAPTER 7

LSD - LOVE POTION #9

"I held my nose, I closed my eyes
I took a drink
I couldn't tell if it was day or night
I started kissing everything in sight"
                LOVE POTION #9 - THE CLOVERS

"Purple haze all in my brain
Lately things just don't seem the same
Actin' funny but I don't know why
'Scuse me while I kiss the sky"
          PURPLE HAZE - THE JIMI HENDRIX EXPERIENCE

One of the most powerful and enigmatic substances to ever invade the human consciousness is the hallucinogenic drug, D- lysergic acid diethylamide tartrate, more commonly known as LSD- 25. What is LSD? To put it briefly and succinctly, LSD is in essence a pharmaceutical doorway into another reality, but the reality to which I refer has nothing in common with the static reality of normal everyday experience which is governed by its Creator (the God I now gratefully and respectfully call Father); it is, instead, a shifting, distorted, and often frightening reality governed by the *other* god; the god of this corrupted world system in which we now live.

In the Holy Bible, the scripture passage of II Cor. 4:3,4 states that the "*god of this world*" blinds the minds of its inhabitants who willingly refuse to believe in the Gospel of the Lord Jesus Christ. Satan, the Dragon, the mind blinder is the other "god" of whom I speak. He is the governor of the land of false reality.

Tantric Hindu yogi achieving Samadhi, the tantric state, at the point of death when the spirit exits the body by choice in this case never to return. Notice the light streaming out of the top of the head, and the small ball of concentrated light at the pinacle of the ray. Hindus believe that the spirit leaves the body from the 7th or "crown" chakra (spiritual energy center). Meditators take a good look. This is what yoga can do for you.!

The God of the Bible warns his people to stay far away from *ALL* illicit drugs, especially those used in sorcery because He knows very well the dangerous doorways of demonic deception they can open up within the human soul.

Let me explain what I mean. During Hindu meditation, an adept yogi will usually experience many of the same visions, wild bright lights, strange etheric sounds, and encounters with spirit-beings that many people have described after ingesting LSD...An ex-Hindu Brahmin priest explains:

> "Often while in deep meditation the gods became visible and talked with me. At times I seemed to be transported by **astral projection** to distant planets or to worlds in other dimensions. It would be years before I would learn that such experiences were being duplicated in laboratories under watchful eyes of parapsychologists through the use of hypnosis and **LSD**."[1]
>
> RABI MAHARAJ - AUTHOR, EVANGELIST

Kali, in the annihilation aspect Shakti, the goddess of death. Notice the cobra snake around her neck and the necklace and waistband of severed heads and arms about her person. Also notice the extended tongue, done in true Gene Simmons fashion. Obviously yours is not a new pose Gene!

Ingestion of LSD is, in fact, a physiological shortcut to the same experiences that yoga and meditation have been providing to the followers of the eastern Hindu religions for thousands of years. Even the father of LSD Dr. Albert Hofmann, who discovered the drug in 1943, says LSD led him into Eastern Hindu meditation.

Ex-Beatle, George Harrison, is well aware of this fact. His past excursion into devil worship in the temple of Kali (the Hindu goddess of death) in Calcutta, India was actually instigated by this powerful drug. He told *Rolling Stone* magazine in 1987:

> "When I was younger with the effects of the L.S.D. that *OPENED* [interesting choice of words!] something up inside me in 1966, a flood of other thoughts came into my head, which **led me to the yogis.**"[2]

Harrison, however, was not the only Rock & Roll musician to experience the Hindu darkness brought about by the ingestion of LSD. It was also experienced by an "Animal".

ERIC MEETS KALI

Another musician to personally connect the LSD experience with Hinduism was Eric Burdon, from the British rock and blues group, The Animals. His experience is so supportive of the hypothesis of this book, when I discovered it I almost jumped out of my chair with excitement. This account is one of the most powerful correlations between LSD and Hinduism I have ever heard. Let's let Eric tell us of his unusual encounter. In his autobiography entitled, I Used To Be An Animal, But I'm All Right Now, he writes:

"There was a lot of acid going about and my world was one of visions and hallucinations...I was doing regular LSD sessions. Serious ones at a mutual friend's house. During most of these acid sessions, taken either as a group or separately, we exchanged ideas. With the Dodger, The Pill, Brian Epstein [The Beatles' manager!!], Zoot Money, and Hilton Valentine. We'd all purposefully stay at home, meditate and exchange opinions and ideas about what we had encountered.

There was this heavy session going on in the Dodgers house one night. In attendance was Barry Jenkins, The Dodger, Andy, his Indian mate and myself. Andy [Summers, the guitarist for the Police--Small world isn't it?] was creating a mural on seven panels which explained the birth of the world as taught by KRISHNA. In the end-panel amongst the trees and foliage, was a princess who was KALI, goddess of DEATH and destruction. One night, after staring at this woman emerging out of the foliage in the last panel, under the influence of the drug, I began to have visions of an idyllic female...After staring at the goddess in the mural I fell into a deep coma on the floor and was surrounded by the rest of the people in the room. We all reached, under the influence of the hallucinogenic, the same level. We could talk and describe where we were

and discuss the place we arrived at. Andy's voice said 'Can anybody see the staircase?' He told me to climb up it. I was thrust into a sky, filled with bright shining stars, which turned into eyes. 'Go for one', Andy instructed. I sought out one eye, and moved right into it. Then I came face to face with KALI. I was covered in a void. Darkness, darkness. Then a voice asked what right I had to come there and disturb KALI. 'I'm just a man', I said. 'And what makes you think you're man enough to disturb me while I'm making love?' 'My ego tells me that if I have a chance to change the world, I have the power to make that change.' 'Ah, so you need answers', said Kali. 'If you want information you have to make me a gift.'
I didn't know which world I was in. My own was left behind me. 'I can't see you. You've already taken my sight. What more do you want?' She laughed a wicked, cruel laugh in the darkness. 'How much are you willing to give?' 'My life.' I said. **My life was sucked out of me.** I was Gonzo. Melted to the floor. **DEAD.**"[3]

It is clear by this incredible information that Eric Burdon had obviously stepped over the same line into spiritual "death" and communion with evil spirits that the yogis and shamans consistently attempt to cross, and LSD was just the ticket he needed for the "trip".

It is imperative to remember that drug use was, and is, still quite prevalent, as we mentioned in an earlier chapter, in the lives of the yogis, shamans, and voodoo priests.

Ingesting mind-altering drugs such as LSD, psilocybin ("magic mushrooms"), peyote, opium and hashish is meant for one purpose and one purpose alone; to break down the mind's God-given legitimate perception of reality, and produce an altered state of consciousness necessary for a more effective contact with the demonic spirit world. Once a person, shaman or not, takes that step, their understanding of reality and truth can be irreversibly manipulated, altered, and damaged.

The effect of this spiritual damage has yet to be fully understood; yet we have for years been constantly bombarded with music created by people who have seen the world through a self- induced psychedelic fog.

The lives and philosophies of a multitude of well known Rock & Roll musicians, just as in the case of the yogis and shamans, have been tremendously altered by a simple ingestion of mind expanding drugs, the most common one being "acid" (LSD).

The Beatles; The Rolling Stones; The Who, David Bowie; The Moody Blues; Pink Floyd; The Cream; The Jefferson Airplane; Iron Butterfly; Country Joe & The Fish; The Eagles; The Grateful Dead; Lynyrd Skynyrd; The Byrds; The Mamas & The Papas; Janis Joplin; Jimi Hendrix Experience; Jim Morrison and The Doors; John McLaughlin and the Mahavishnu Orchestra; Donovan; Ozzy Osbourne and Black Sabbath; Eric Burdon & The Animals; The Police; The Ramones; Santana; Moby Grape; Crosby, Stills, Nash and Young; Fleetwood Mac; Bob Dylan; Arlo Guthrie; Quicksilver Messenger Service; Mitch Ryder; Love; and even, believe it or not, Elvis Presley; Little Richard; and the Beach Boys, were all involved once, or in some cases hundreds of times with this reality rending, spirit shattering, soul stealing drug called LSD.

If an in-depth investigation were conducted evaluating the belief systems of all the musicians and the groups just mentioned you would, no doubt, see the universal effect that this drug has had on their perceptions of life, truth, religion, and most importantly, their concepts of God.

At one time or another, most of these musicians have admitted to at least some interest in the occult, as well as sharing a belief in reincarnation, a definitive Hindu teaching.

Though they may not all agree on how they feel regarding the occult, amazingly enough they *ALL* agree on one thing: their opinion of Christianity. To these Rock & Roll shamans, as far as the adoption of a personal belief system is concerned, Christianity is the bottom rung on the spiritual ladder. Eastern mysticism was, and still is, held by most in much higher esteem. (Rolling Stone Mick Jagger and his common law wife Jerry Hall have both recently announced their belief and acceptance of Hinduism as their own religion.)

Through the leadership of these Rock & Roll gurus of the 1960's and 70's, America has taken one giant step backward. This retrogression has resulted in producing the same occult bondage and spiritual DEMONIC MANIPULA-TION which, to this day, still blinds and binds many of the pagan cultures in far off lands to the devils they continue to worship and serve.

If you want to see the Dragon smile...just worship him. Oh...but don't make the fatal mistake of thinking he really cares about you. Just remember...HE WOULD RATHER...*SEE YOU DEAD!!*

Heartbeat of the Dragon

CHAPTER 8

CHILDREN OF THE BEAST

"I may be a **Black Magician,** but I'm a bloody great one!"[1]
THE GREAT BEAST - ALEISTER CROWLEY
CROWLEY'S DIARY, 1923

60 years later. . . .

"...so come now *children of the beast* be strong..."
SHOUT AT THE DEVIL - MÖTLEY CRÜE, 1983

Some of the most popular and influential groups and musicians of our era have read, taught, and emulated the theologies, philosophies, and lifestyles of some of the most evil and confused men and women to ever walk this earth. The influence these musicians have had on their Rock & Roll proteges, and the public at large, as well as the *true* source of their inspiration are the subjects we will now continue to examine.

One man who was briefly mentioned in a previous chapter is black magic satanist Aleister Crowley. Who was this man and why should we be so concerned about him? These are the questions that we are about to answer.

Considering the fact that the autobiographical account of Crowley's life, which I have in my possession, entitled, The Confessions of Aleister Crowley, is over 1000 pages in length, as well as the fact that all this information, for the purpose of this writing, must be condensed into just a few pages, let us now begin our rather brief excursion into the sordid life of the man they called "The Great Beast".

ALEISTER CROWLEY - THE BEAST 666

A young Aleister Crowley posing with magick ritual paraphenalia

Edward Alexander Crowley was born in Leamington, England on October 12, 1875 into a family of religious extremists. The Crowley family were members of a strict Christian sect called the Plymouth Brethren.

Early in his Christian life, the only literature he was encouraged to read was the Bible. Although he enjoyed his Christian home life, much of what he read in the Bible left him unimpressed. There were certain parts, however, which seemed to draw most of his attention. He found reading about the Kingdom of Heaven and the angelic hosts much less exciting and interesting than reading about the biblical villians of the Book of Revelation: the Dragon, the False Prophet, the Beast, and the Scarlet Woman.

Young Alick, as he was called, would often even fantasize about what it would be like to undergo the torments of Hell, identifying himself in his fantasy as the

Beast whose number is 666. These anti-Christ fantasies were the foundation on which his future life would eventually be built.

Though his father, Edward Crowley, was a member of the Plymouth Brethren, he was also a brewer by trade. Selling *Crowley Ale* is how he made the family fortune. This was rather unusual, however, considering the stand of the Plymouth Brethren condemning the consumption of alcohol. The Crowley family couldn't drink it themselves, but they could sure make money by selling it to others! This hypocrisy did not escape the observant eye of the elder Crowley's young son. That, and similar hypocritical behavior by others in their Christian sect, such as severe beatings by the schoolmaster, and homosexual advances from his "Christian" classmates eventually drove young Crowley far away from the God these people worshiped, as well as the book they revered.

His father, the main Christian influence in his life, died when he was only 11 years old. This gave him a perfect opportunity to explore the world outside; a world filled with everything the Bible taught as evil.

Early in his life Edward Alexander, as a result of his Plymouth Brethren association, developed a strong hatred for Jesus Christ and Christianity. By the time he was 14 years old, he had already made his decision to walk totally away from God; by the time he reached his early twenties he changed his given name to Aleister and embarked on a journey into a life of debauchery and excess that would span half a century and most of the continents of the world.

His mother had called him "The Great Beast of Revelation whose number is 666", a title which actually pleased him greatly. He decided to show her and everyone else that he could definitely live up to the name. His reputation for corruption was unparalleled in his day. The press in many countries called him "the wickedest man in the world". Drugs like heroin and cocaine; bisexuality, sodomy, blood sacrifice, black magic, and just about any kind of sexual perversion you could imagine began to envelope his sordid life.

Early in his dark career, Crowley quickly arose as a leader in one of the most well known occult organizations of his day called The Hermetic Order of the Golden Dawn. This secret order embraced a virtual menagerie of mystical beliefs and practices, extracting many aspects of their religion from such esoteric groups as Theosophy, Rosicrucianism, Gnosticism, and Kabbalism, as well as many other anti-Christian belief systems.

From blood sacrifice, to black magic, to drug use, to extreme acts of perversion including bestiality and the consumption of human feces, Crowley and his

Upper left: Aleister Crowley, 1910, wearing the headdress of Egyptian pagan god Horus. Notice the eye in the center of the triangle of light. Also notice the position of the thumbs of his hands in a turned up position. This represents the sign of the horns of Pan. Upper right: Crowley's girlfriend or "scarlet worman" Leila Waddell. Notice the tatoo in the center of her chest. That is Crowley's "Mark of the Beast." Lower left: Crowley self-portrait. Notice the medallion which says "To Mega Therion 666" it translates "The Great Beast 666." Lower right: Crowley toward the end of his years working on his magick wand.

followers were unabashedly following the path of black Tantra. His writings on these subjects have become some of the most popular in the occult world today.

Aleister Crowley also taught what he called the beneficial aspects of working with the demonic. He knew many of the demons by name, and actually instructed his close disciples in the fine art of becoming DEMON POSSESSED!

Everything Crowley did was purposefully anti-Christian, and in most of his writings, he made his hatred for Jesus Christ and Christianity very clear. He wrote such statements as:

"I do not wish to argue that the **doctrines of Jesus**, they and they alone, have degraded the world to it's present condition. I take it that Christianity is not only the cause but the symptom of slavery."[2]

He also railed:

"That religion they call Christianity; the devil they honor they call God. I accept these definitions, as a poet must do, if he is to be at all intelligible to his age, and it is their God and their religion that I *hate* and will *DESTROY*."[3]

As his delusions of grandeur grew, so did the illusions of his messianic mission. He decided to start his own religion. Now called the Church of Thelema, it was originally called Crowlianity, with Aleister himself being the new self-appointed messiah. Why not? He said himself that he was "the light, the savior of the world".

Now prepare yourself for a real shock. This man, called "the Great Beast", or the "Master Therion" who had purposefully immersed himself in evil, has touched the lives of more Rock & Roll musicians than you can possibly imagine. His law of life, "Do What Thou Wilt", has been readily adopted as marching orders by Rock & Rollers all over this planet. Here is a brief list of just some of those to whom Crowley and his writings have been a source of influence and inspiration:

1. The Beatles

2. Ozzy Osbourne & Black Sabbath
3. The Rolling Stones
4. Marc Bolan -- T. Rex
5. David Bowie
6. Graham Bond -- Graham Bond Organisation
   Holy Magick Band
7. Jim Morrison & The Doors
8. Sting -- formerly with The Police
9. Jimmy Page -- Led Zeppelin
10. Daryl Hall -- Hall & Oates
11. Tom G. Warrior -- Celtic Frost
12. Stiv Bators -- Lords of the New Church
13. Nige Rockett -- Onslaught
14. King Diamond -- formerly with Mercyful Fate
15. Genesis P. Orridge -- Psychic T.V.
16. Bruce Dickinson -- Iron Maiden
17. Glenn Danzig -- the Misfits
    Samhain
    Danzig

Every single person and group mentioned has exhibited a strong hatred for Jesus Christ, the Bible, and Christianity. I'm quite sure this is not a mere coincidence.

At his funeral in 1947, Aleister Crowley, ever true to his reputation, had his followers read the words from his poem, "Hymn To Pan", a demon god that Crowley worshiped. Part of his epitaph read as follows:

> "I *rave* and I *rape* and I *rip* and I *rend*
> Everlasting world without end"[4]
> HYMN TO PAN - ALEISTER CROWLEY

This, my friends, is the man whose philosophy of life many of yesterday's and today's Rock & Roll musicians wholeheartedly follow: "DO WHAT THOU WILT SHALL BE THE WHOLE OF THE LAW"[5]...the first commandment of Aleister Crowley.

This statement, however, did not originate in the mind of Aleister Crowley. It was actually imparted to him by an entity calling itself Aiwass who appeared to Crowley during one of his "magick" sessions. Crowley believed this spirit-being to be his "holy" guardian angel.

Now, if we trace this same statement, "DO WHAT THOU WILT", back to its origin, we might just possibly find it slithering off the tongue of a serpent who had once been possessed by *another* angel with a different name...Lucifer. Where did all this take place? In a garden called "EDEN".

How has an association with the teachings of Aleister Crowley affected the lives of the musicians on our list. In the case of the Beatles we already know. What about the others? Let's take a closer look and see.

Heartbeat of the Dragon

CHAPTER 9

THE MAGICK OF LED ZEPPELIN - STAIRWAY TO HADES

Led Zeppelin was, without question, one of the most popular and influential bands to ever make an appearance upon the rock music scene. Their inception in 1968 was actually intended to be a newly reformed "Yardbirds", with Jimmy Page on lead guitar, but not long after Page formed his new band with drummer, John Bonham; bass player and keyboardist, John Paul Jones; and lead vocalist, Robert Plant, the "Yardbirds" name was dropped and another name was chosen.

The idea for the name, Led Zeppelin, as the story goes, actually came as somewhat of a fluke when future road manager Richard Cole overheard a conversation between Keith Moon and John Entwistle, two members of the Who. They were drunk, moaning and complaining about how tired they were of playing with Pete Townsend and Roger Daltrey, and said if they ever left the Who they would like to start a band with Jimmy Page (at that time a Yardbird) and Stevie Winwood (singer and keyboardist for the band Traffic). As the alcohol induced banter continued, their evaluation of such a corroboration developed into bleak cynicism. Imagining no hope of success for such a group, they decided to call this imaginary band Lead Zeppelin, because, they quipped, it would probably go over "like a lead balloon". This gave them both a big laugh; but Cole later that night told Jimmy Page about the incident and about the name that had so amused the two disgruntled members of the Who. Page liked it, and not long afterward the new Yardbirds became instead...Led Zeppelin.

THE PAGE/CROWLEY CONNECTION

An entire book could easily be written on this group and just their occult involvement; but for this one we will mainly be examining their ties with Aleister Crowley.

Sex, drugs, Hinduism, and occultism filled the life of Aleister Crowley; these same subjects also seemed to dominate the lives and music of Jimmy Page and his band as well.

Sex, in particular, as with Crowley, was their major preoccupation. From the music, to the motel room escapades (some including bestiality), their reputation for licentiousness was well known.

Songs full of sexual innuendo recorded on their second album, such as "Living Loving Maid", "The Lemon Song", and their first hit single, "Whole Lotta Love", left no doubt in the mind of the listener that sex provided the inspiration for much of Zeppelin's music.

At some time in 1970, however, the interest of Led Zeppelin guitarist Jimmy Page shifted from sex to the occult. This transition took place after an encounter with Kenneth Anger, a black magician, one of the founding members of the Church of Satan, and a disciple of Aleister Crowley. Page got so excited after hearing about Crowley and his magical powers, he immediately went out and purchased Crowley's old home called Boleskine House, located on the shores of the famous Loch Ness. After the purchase was completed, Page had a known satanist decorate the inside with ritualistic occult symbols and assumed occupancy.

Around this same time, the Crowley influence in Led Zeppelin began to appear. Clearly, the connecting link between Led Zeppelin and Aleister Crowley was Jimmy Page. He became so enamored by the teachings of Crowley that a multitude of the first pressings of the Led Zeppelin III album, featuring their second hit single, "The Immigrant Song", were all graced with a special inscription which was scratched into the vinyl band just outside the record's center label. What was the message that Jimmy Page had been compelled to communicate to the Led Zeppelin fans? Simply this: *"DO WHAT THOU WILT"*, Crowley's law.

Not until the fourth album was released, however, did the music begin to reflect the Page/Crowley connection in a much more tangible way. This album,

Figure of hermit from tarot taken from inside cover of LZ IV album. Notice hexagram or six-pointed star in lantern.

Led Zeppelin IV, was the one that really held the key to revealing the source of their new musical inspiration.

Along with hats, canes, two ritual robes, multitudes of manuscripts and books written by Crowley, and lots of other Crowleyana, Jimmy also became the proud owner of Crowley's Tarot deck. (Tarot cards are used by diviners in their attempt to foretell the future. All forms of divination and experimentation in the occult are cursed by God. See Deut. 18:9-14.)

On the inside cover of the Led Zeppelin IV (or Zoso) album is a picture of a figure from one of the cards in the Tarot deck. The figure on the card is called the Hermit. The Hermit symbolizes occult power and the light of "truth". In his hand is a lantern containing a six-pointed star adopted from tantric Hinduism called a HEXAGRAM, which is the source of this light. In the occult this light has a name. It is called LUCIFER.

Now, if you remember correctly, in the first chapter of this book, we discussed this name. It was the original name given by God (Isa. 14:12) to the angel who became the DRAGON.

Just like the pentagram (another occult symbol we will discuss in the next chapter), the hexagram is a symbol that has been used throughout history by black magicians like Crowley. Jimmy Page, with this album cover, as well as his portion of the Led Zeppelin movie, "The Song Remains The Same", was clearly prompting his listeners to investigate the occult. But the music on this album...that was the *real* story.

THE DESCENDING STAIRWAY

One song on this same Led Zeppelin IV album, which suddenly made Led Zeppelin a household name, was destined to become the most requested song in Rock & Roll radio history. It is called "Stairway to Heaven".

Much of the lyrical content of this quickly written, Dragon- inspired song was taken from either the teachings of Crowley, his demon companions, or both. Let me explain.

When Robert Plant wrote the lyrics for this song he said it was as if the pen was moving across the paper by itself, *almost automatically.* In the occult this phenomenon is called "automatic writing".

"Automatic writing" is produced when a person acting as the medium allows his or her body to be temporarily controlled or possessed by an alien spirit who is desiring to communicate. The medium holds a pencil or pen, relaxes, and the spirit does the writing.

This flowing type of automatic writing has been practiced by occultists all over the world for centuries; from Emanuel Swedenborg, the long ago deceased leader of the cult known as the Church of the New Jerusalem, who through automatic writing received "new" interpretations of Bible scriptures; to Ruth Montgomery, author and self-proclaimed "herald" of the New Age who regularly communicates with disincarnate spirits and practices both automatic writing and typewriting.

The lyrics to "Stairway to Heaven" written by Plant, seem to have originated in very much the same way.

On a close examination of the lyrics to this song, a very strong Crowleyan influence can be detected. One particular line in the song explains exactly what I mean. The line says:

"There's a feeling I get
When I look **to the west**
And my spirit is crying for leaving"

It took some extensive research to find out what this line really means, but with the Lord's help it has finally been discovered. If you were unfamiliar with Aleister Crowley's book called <u>MAGICK: In Theory and Practice</u>, this song lyric would mean very little, but the secret meaning behind this very obscure line will now be brought into the light of truth. Here is the TRUE meaning of these lyrics.

On page 39 of Crowley's (black) Magick book it reveals that looking "to the WEST" is part of a mystical initiation ceremony for any neophyte or beginner desiring to be a member of Aleister Crowley's secret occult order. It states:

"After further purification and consecration he [speaking of the initiate] is allowed for one moment to see the **Lord of the WEST**, and **gains courage** to persist."[1]

Let me explain what is taking place during this ceremony. The initiate first allows himself to be bound and blindfolded, which is symbolic admission of his total spiritual ignorance and incapability. He is to forget all that he has ever been taught concerning the knowledge of spiritual things. He is then purified, consecrated, and led into the temple where he walks around the room in a specific geometrical pattern. This walking is called his **mystical *circumambulation***. He then stops his walk, and facing in the direction of the WEST where his blindfold is briefly removed, he is allowed to see someone called the "Lord of the West". Facing the direction of the west is extremely important. This is meant to spiritually strengthen him to continue with the ceremony and become more deeply involved with his occult training.

Crowley continues the explanation of this occult ceremony. He further states regarding the initiate:

"IN THE WEST HE GAINS ENERGY."[2]

Now, you can clearly see that the "feeling I get when I look to the west" sung by Robert Plant in Led Zeppelin's song, "Stairway to Heaven", is obviously occult power and energy received from partaking in Crowley's magickal initiation ceremony. It is given to the initiate by the spirit powers that energized Crowley and his followers.

Jimmy Page, being a student of Crowley's teachings, was undoubtedly well aware of this fact. Robert Plant, who admittedly, at one time, held a fascination for Celtic magic, just as Jimmy, may also have been privy to this information; but whether they knew it or not, it is very clear that the same demonic spirit who inspired both writings: Crowley's "MAGICK" book and Led Zeppelin's magick song, "Stairway to Heaven"; knew this similarity existed.

There are also other lines in the song which mention "the PIPER", such as "The piper's calling you to join him" and "The piper will lead us to reason". This term, "the piper", is a clear reference to the pagan god PAN. Pan, a god of sexuality and lust is pictured as half man half goat; a cloven hoofed satyr who plays a reed pipe flute. Hence the reference to "the piper". Jimmy Page, who helped write "Stairway", also knew that of all the gods Crowley worshiped, Pan was his favorite.

Let me make one very clear statement at this point. The song, "Stairway to Heaven", continues to saturate the airwaves of Rock & Roll radio stations to this day. The line...

> "There's a lady who's sure all that glitters is gold
> And she's buying a stairway to heaven"

...is nothing short of a master deception. Heaven, contrary to what an occultist would teach, is not a state of mind or a higher plane of existence; and you cannot *buy*, or for that matter earn your way in with "good" works, religious church participation, meditation, or anything else. The only price that God will accept to assure your entry into Heaven (which by the way IS A REAL PLACE) is your covering of the cleansing BLOOD OF JESUS CHRIST, which He shed for your sins on the cross. The Bible explains this very clearly:

> *"But God commendeth his love toward us, in that, while we were yet sinners, Christ died for us. Much more then, being now*

justified by HIS BLOOD, we shall BE SAVED FROM WRATH
THROUGH HIM."

Romans 5:8,9

God spent His wrath and judgment against sin *ON THE BODY OF JESUS*
CHRIST instead of on *YOU.*

Heaven is a place where the departed spirits of those who have accepted Christ
as their Savior now live. The ONLY WAY for you to get into Heaven is to ask
Jesus Christ into your life, reject the darkness, confess your sins, and follow
God's WORD with all your heart. Jimmy Page won't tell you that, because he
doesn't know it, BUT I WILL!!!...because *I DO.*

THE QUEEN OF LIFE

One more rather tragic, but nevertheless intriguing fact, I discovered concerning the Led Zeppelin IV album is almost too ironic to believe; but it vividly
reveals what a close involvement with the music of Led Zeppelin can foment.

The only person to ever record on a Led Zeppelin track, besides the immediate
members of the group, is mentioned on the inside album jacket of Led Zep IV.
Her name is Sandy Denny. Robert invited her to do a duet with him on one of
their songs entitled, "The Battle Of Evermore"; the song just preceding "Stairway to Heaven" on Side One. The true irony lies in the fact that Sandy Denny,
a former classmate of Jimmy Page at Kensington Art School, is no longer with
us. She died in a freak accident that took place in her home when she fell down
her own stairway! She later died of injuries sustained as a result of the
fall...Irony indeed.

In a poll held by the British music newspaper "Melody Maker", Sandy Denny
was voted England's top female vocalist in 1970 and 1971 which was the same
year that Zeppelin released their fourth album. They invited her to sing on their
record; an honor never before bestowed on any other person. The Stephen Davis
bio of the Zeps mentions not only the song she sang, but the character roles the
two balladeers assumed in the song. Davis writes:

"Sandy Denny, the bell-clear soprano from Fairport Convention,
came in [to the studio] to sing the haunting duet/playlet in 'The

Above: Cover of "Houses of the Holy" album by Led Zeppelin. Naked little girls climbing a stone "Stairway to Heaven".
Below: Inside cover of "Houses of the Holy". Crowley type bald figure offers child sacrifice to the "light."

Battle of Evermore', playing the Queen of Life to Robert's Prince of Peace"[3]

Ms. Denny would have done a lot better to have turned down this invitation from Robert Plant and sought out the TRUE Prince of Peace. Had she done this maybe then she would have been spared the same fate that has also befallen Karac Plant, Robert's now dead son, and John Bonham (Led Zeppelin's deceased drummer). Tragically, she also discovered any involvement with Led Zeppelin can carry a heavy price tag. The Dragon and his angels probably had a good laugh as they watched the "Queen of Life" tumble headlong down the stairs...not a "Stairway to Heaven", but a stairway leading to a very different destination. Without Jesus, the stairway of death always leads to just one place...Hell. Sandy Denny, the only person to have ever recorded with the mighty Led Zeppelin, quite ironically, on the same album containing their mega hit "Stairway To Heaven", is now DEAD.

Zeppelin's next *unholy* album, "Houses of the Holy", also showed a clear reference to Aleister Crowley. On the inside album cover is a picture of a bald, naked man raising a female child above his head as an offering to a light streaming down from the wall of a mysterious looking castle. It is a symbolic representation of ritual child sacrifice. Crowley, bald for much of his life, was reputed to teach and practice what he called "sex magick" which was always performed in the nude. The reference here to Aleister Crowley on this Led Zeppelin album cover could not be more absolute.

The Page/Crowley connection continues on throughout Zeppelin's musical career. On their "Physical Graffiti" album are two more songs that express Crowley sentiment very well. If you remember correctly, Crowley hated Jesus Christ. On the song, "In My Time of Dying", Robert Plant not only mocks Jesus and salvation, singing the lines:

> "Meet me Jesus, meet me
> Meet me in the middle of the air
> If my wings should fail me, Lord
> Please meet me with another pair"

but he also mocks the Kingdom of Heaven singing, "St. Peter won't you let me in" and "Gabriel let me blow your horn". Another song on the "Graffiti" album entitled "Kashmir" is nothing short of a heavy endorsement of Hinduism, which, as we mentioned earlier, played a key role in the formation of Crowley's belief system.

As you can see, not only in the music, but also in the spirit, Jimmy Page is a follower of Aleister Crowley. God help poor "Pagey". He is about to find out that the occult lie he has been promoting for far too many years is *cursed* by the Living God. I only hope and pray he doesn't find it out too late. Jesus died for Jimmy Page too. He can still escape the destiny of the, lost that has already claimed his bandmate John Bonham and his mentor Aleister Crowley; and so can *YOU*, but remember this: Time is running out. The *LAST* thing the Dragon wants, is for you to escape his destructive grasp by accepting Jesus Christ **NOW**; he would rather have you wait...**FOREVER!**

Though I don't have adequate space in this short book to go into great detail concerning the lives of the people and groups mentioned in the last chapter who are connected with Aleister Crowley, suffice it to say their stories are very much the same: filled with deception, destruction, excess, and in more than one instance...**DEATH.**

Ozzy Osbourne, who said that Crowley was "the phenomenon of his time", and wrote a song about him entitled, "Mr Crowley", is irrevocably demon possessed (excluding his willingness to petition God for salvation and deliverance through the death and resurrection of Jesus Christ). He has admitted in many interviews I have read, that he is not in control of his life. The choking incident and recent death threat by Ozzy against his wife Sharon would prove this to be true.

Beatle - John Lennon, who put Crowley's face on their Sgt. Pepper album cover, and hated Jesus and Christianity, probably as much as Crowley...is **DEAD.**

The Rolling Stones, who were for a while tutored by a black magician in the teachings and practices of Aleister Crowley, have continued throughout their dark career to use black magic and voodoo sorcery in their lives and music.

So far, the only eternal casualty has been the death of founding guitarist Brian Jones. But even with that tragedy under their belts, the Stones have learned nothing from their past. One of the songs on their recent smash hit album, "Steel Wheels", entitled "Continental Drift", uses recordings from the very same Voodoo musicians of Joujouka whom Brian felt had placed the curse on him that eventually resulted in his strange death in July of 1969. The Stones are still using Voodoo...Brian Jones, however, is **DEAD.**

Sting poses adorned with ritual paint job. Standing along side of South American Indian Chief Raoni, chief of the Kayapo Indians of Brazil. Sting says the highlight of his trip to the rain forest was meeting a shaman named Tacuma who was in the process of recovering after being struck by lightning.

<u>Sting</u>, besides spending many hours reading Crowley's books, as well as embracing the philosophy of "Synchronicity" developed by the heavily demonized, occultist/psychologist Carl Jung, has also ventured into the Amazon rain forest of South America. While there, he ended up dancing around naked for several days in native *shamanic* ceremonies dedicated to devil gods.

<u>Marc Bolan</u> of T. Rex fame lived for two years with a black magician in Paris, France where he practiced black magic. He said his magic was responsible for his popularity and musical success. Popularity and success might have seemed worth selling his soul for at the time, but Marc Bolan now knows this was a big mistake! He is now the beneficiary of his reward for serving darkness...eternal separation from God. He is also **DEAD**.

<u>Jim Morrison</u>, the Rock & Roll shaman who shared Crowley's philosophy and ideals, posed with a bust of Crowley for a band promo picture which was used on the back of the "Doors 13" album cover. He was also married to a witch in a ceremony where they drank their mingled BLOOD from a chalice while they INVOKED the GODDESS...Morrison is **DEAD**.

Above: Back of "Doors 13" album cover with group posing around a bust of Aleister Crowley.
Below: Close up of Jim Morrison posing with Crowley bust.

Graham Bond, not only claimed to be Crowley's son, but also formed his "HOLY MAGICK" band dedicated to Crowley and his magick. He was cursed by a black magician who also followed the teachings of Crowley...Bond is **DEAD.**

Stiv Bators, the lead singer of The Lords of The New Church, who sang songs with lyrics such as, "I heard the Devil curse/I recognized my name", and "DO WHAT THOU WILT/This is the law" (Crowley's code), was hit by a car in Paris, France on Monday, June 4, 1990. The Dragon has just recently collected another of his servants' souls...Bators is also **DEAD.**

The others, mentioned in the previous chapter: Bowie, Danzig, Dickinson, and the rest; well, they haven't learned their lesson yet either. I hope and pray they will come to an understanding of this fact **soon:** The Dragon DOES NOT PLAY GAMES!!! **HE KILLS!** But he also deceives...very...very...well.

Heartbeat of the Dragon

CHAPTER 10

TWINKLE TWINKLE EVIL STAR: THE LEGACY OF THE PENTAGRAM

"But this is now my aeon, and my PENTAGRAM is again to be pure in its splendor. Cast aside the corruptions, that the PENTA-GRAM of SET [SATAN] may shine forth. Let ALL WHO SEEK ME NEVER BE WITHOUT IT, OPENLY AND WITH PRIDE for *BY IT I SHALL KNOW THEM.*"[1]

SET (through satanist high priest Lt. Col. Michael Aquino)
BOOK OF COMING FORTH BY NIGHT

If you are at all knowledgeable about the occult it is almost certain you have heard of a geometrical configuration called the pentagram. The PENTAGRAM is a five-pointed star drawn within the boundaries of a circle (although the circle is not always necessary) used by many people involved in occultism today. It is considered by some to be a powerful demonic symbol used specifically for the purpose of evil. But by others, such as witches, who also employ its use, it is reputed to hold no malevolent properties whatsoever. What is the pentagram used for; what powers, if any, does using it evoke; and what happens to those who use or wear this occult symbol? These are the questions that will be answered in this chapter.

THE KALI YANTRA

All throughout the composition of this book, our research has uncovered unusual and distinct connections between Hinduism, the occult, and Rock &

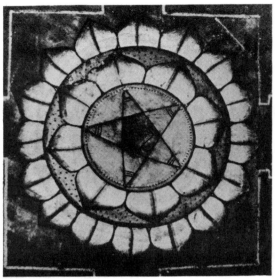

Shyama (Kali) Yantra painting from the 18th century. Notice the pentagram in the center.
Kali is the Hindu goddess of death.

Roll. In examining the subject of the pentagram, the connection once again remains unbroken.

In a book entitled The Tantric Way, I was amazed to find a pentagram at the center of another geometrical configuration called a YANTRA. Hindus believe that a person who meditates on the pattern of a yantra will either experience a change in consciousness, or the deity it represents will actually make contact with the worshiper.

After a further investigation of the yantra containing the pentagram at its center, I was even more intrigued to find out the name of the deity this particular yantra represents. The yantra is called the SHYAMA yantra, SHYAMA being another name for the female Hindu deity named KALI the goddess of *DEATH*, that we mentioned earlier in chapter 6 in connection with George Harrison and Eric Burdon. This Kali yantra that I discovered while in the process of researching information for this book dates back to the 1700's. So as you can now see, the PENTAGRAM was being used in the worship of Kali, the DEATH GODDESS, as early as the 18th century; but I have also recently discovered this symbol is even more ancient.

High priest of Set, Lt. Col. Michael Aquino and wife, Lilith, posing beneath their pentagram.

A very good friend of mine, Dr. Suresh Chander Verma, a former Hindu priest raised in India, who has now become a born again Christian and servant of the Lord Jesus Christ, told me that he has seen this Kali (pentagram) yantra in Hindu art and architecture dating back thousands of years. Since Kali *is* the Hindu goddess of *DEATH*, it should now be quite evident that the pentagram, which çan be seen at the heart of her yantra, has always been, and to this day continues to be, associated with evil, occultism, and DEATH.

Let's now follow the pentagram down a more contemporary trail and discover if this observation and evaluation is valid.

THE TEMPLE OF SET

We began this chapter with a passage taken from a book written by Lt. Col. Michael Aquino. Aquino, a former member of Anton LaVey's Church of Satan, being disenchanted by what he perceived as insincerity by his former mentor, became the high priest of his own satanic church called The Temple of Set. (Set is an ancient Egyptian god which represents Satan.) It is located in his home in San Francisco, California.

I have no doubt at all that Satan, whom Aquino knows as SET, was using Michael Aquino when he wrote the statement that opened this chapter. It was taken from Aquino's book entitled, The Book of Coming Forth by Night, in which he says that the pentagram should be implemented and displayed by anyone who truly desires to serve Set.

If you were to go to the Temple of Set you would see that Aquino obviously holds this symbol in very high esteem. There is one on the wall directly above the chair from which this satanic high priest officiates. It is located above his "throne".

Aquino has also experienced visions of the pentagram while performing satanic rituals in a famous German castle called The Wewelsburg which he visited while he was in Europe. You might be interested to note that this castle was owned by a very well known historical figure. I will let the words of Lt. Col. Aquino explain who the previous owner was. He says:

> "I recounted that HEINRICH HIMMLER had appropriated a Westphalian castle, the Wewelsburg, and had it modified for ritual and **Black Magical** activities of the SS."[2]

Yes, as you just read, Heinrich Himmler, the infamous German Nazi leader and right-hand man of the mad dictator Adolf Hitler, was the owner of the castle -- the place where he had actually performed black magic rituals meant to invoke the powers of darkness who could strengthen the reign of the Nazi SS.

Now the question at hand is, what purpose would Aquino have in this visit? The answer is rather shocking. Why had he gone to Wewelsburg? To perform *HIS OWN* black magic rituals intended to put him in contact with the same spiritual forces that had empowered Adolf Hitler's **Third Reich!** By making this contact he was hoping to enlist these dark forces to help him obtain the same occult power that had launched Nazi Germany on its attempted world conquest. Did his rituals produce the desired results? As a matter of fact, they did. Aquino once again explains in his own words:

> "...upon returning to the medieval museum rooms with the curator,
> I inquired whether I might spend some time in the Hall of the Dead

alone. To my surprise he assented, providing that I sign in the log for the key. I did so, returning alone to the Hall, locked myself in, and undertook what I shall henceforth refer to as the Wewelsburg Working...What emerged from this Working was...First, the suction-like impression of the inflow of certain realizations and kinds of knowledge (accompanied by an almost 'electrical' sort of exhilaration), which seemed to have 'remained dormant' pending an activating 'Working of this sort'."[3]

After being energized (i.e. possessed), he goes on to relate the type of knowledge he was attempting to discover, as well as describing special visions he was given during this experience. He further explains:

"The central figures of the various principal occultisms of the 19th and 20th centuries...ran through my consciousness almost as a pageant. I understood the object of this to be an exposure of contrasts, inaccuracies, and inconsistencies -- a vast, spiraling dialectic designed to clear away the debris of sectarianism and superficiality in the search for the key principles of THE TRUE POWERS OF DARKNESS."[4]

Did the impressions that Aquino received from these powers contain any information concerning the pentagram? Yes, as a matter of fact they did. He received distinct impressions or visions which he would later adopt as the logo for his satanic church. He continues with the description of the vision:

"The Set-headed and -tailed Tcham scepter of ancient Khem rises from the Black Flame, its head at the center of the pentagram. Its tail, against the three central rays of the Flame, forms a "W" denoting the 'Walhalla' or Hall of the Dead at Schloss Wewelsburg, the Great Gate of the Powers of Darkness in our Time."[5]

The last quote you just read makes it quite apparent that the "Powers of Darkness" that Aquino was communicating with during the performance of his "Wewelsburg Working" considered the pentagram a primary occult symbol to be used by their followers. Aquino is definitely one occult practitioner who acknowledges the importance of the pentagram, but he is not the only one, as we will now see.

MORE EVIDENCE

This occult five-pointed star has been used, as we have already seen, in ceremonial magic and worship for virtually thousands of years. Police departments all across the country, day after day, continue to find this symbol connected with satanic crimes and occult murders. Two of the more publicized cases within the last few years are those of California serial killer Richard "NIGHT STALKER" Ramirez, who drew pentagrams on the walls of the homes of some of his murder victims with their own blood; and self-styled satanist, Ricky Kasso, who was very familiar with the use of the pentagram, and was wearing one the night he was arrested for the sacrificial murder of Gary Lauwers. Kasso had stabbed him 17 times and gouged out his eyes. Both Ramirez and Kasso used the pentagram as a symbol of their allegiance to Satan.

The question posed here is, even though these aforementioned people used this symbol, 'Is there really a legitimate connection between the pentagram and the occult?' The answer...without a doubt!

In the book, OCCULT GEOMETRY, by Dr. A.S. Raleigh, written in 1932, the pentagram is clearly mentioned as a symbol widely used and respected in the realm of the occult. He writes:

> "One of the **greatest symbols** is the pentagram the five-pointed star. This is a magical symbol of the greatest potency when correctly drawn with the four points forming a square and the fifth point in midheaven."[6]

What he is explaining is that when the center point of the star points upward it will produce beneficial magic.

Dr. Raleigh goes into great detail in his book to explain that merely *looking* at the pentagram is an excellent means of "greatly intensifying the manasic (mental/spiritual) power in the performance of ceremonial magic", which means it has a profound effect on the spirit of any person continually in contact with the symbol.

Above: Serial murderer Richard "Night Stalker" Ramirez flashes a pentagram on his palm to the reporters and photographers before shouting "Hail Satan" in the courtroom.

Below: 17 year-old demon possessed murderer Ricky Kasso being taken into custody. Kasso never made it to his hearing. He committed suicide by hanging himself with a bed sheet tied to the bars of his holding cell door.

Anton Szandor LaVey, head of the California based Church of Satan and author of the Satanic Bible. Seen here wearing the upside down pentagram complete with lightning bolt.

However, he continues in his evaluation to relate the fact that if the center point of the star is placed in the opposite or downward position, the effect, rather than being beneficial, becomes instead quite detrimental. He continues:

> "In the practice of the black arts, the pentagram is often **reversed** - it will mean mind conquered by the desire, the body, etc., if employed in this way, it is for the purpose of **crushing the mind** of a victim under the weight of desire and physical sensation. It would be employed for the definite purpose of **causing one to go** *INSANE.*"[7]

It is evident by the information given to us in the Occult Geometry book that the pentagram is reputed to be used in *both* "white" and black magic.

Nevertheless, Anton Szandor LaVey, the head of the official Church of Satan and author of the Satanic Bible, places no distinction between *white* and *black* magic whatsoever. His premise declares that they are in essence one and the same. LaVey states that achieving ego gratification and obtaining personal power are the only motivating factors responsible for the actions of the occultist regardless of whether they claim their magic to be BLACK or WHITE. In the Satanic Bible, he writes:

> "There is no difference between 'White' and 'Black' magic, except in the smug hypocrisy, guilt-ridden righteousness, and self-deceit of the 'White' magician himself. In the classical religious tradition, 'White' magic is performed for altruistic, benevolent, and 'good' purposes; while 'Black' magic is used for self-aggrandizement, personal power, and 'evil' purposes."[8]

He finishes his thoughts on the matter with this supportive statement:

> "No one on earth ever pursued occult studies, metaphysics, yoga, or any other 'white light' concept, without ego gratification and personal power as a goal."[9]

The interesting thing about this observation from Anton LaVey is his indictment of *all* occult practices as self-aggrandizing. Selfishness (originated by the Prince of Darkness) is a satanic concept in the truest sense.

Amazingly enough, both Anton LaVey and God's Word agree on the fact that "white" magic does not exist. All magic comes from the same source, and that source is not GOD.

God is very clear on how He views occult practices and those who participate in them. His people are not to be involved in any way with any type of occult behavior. His warning is very clear. The Bible states:

> *"When thou art come into the land which the LORD thy God giveth thee, thou shalt not learn to do after the ABOMINATIONS of those nations. There shall not be found among you anyone that maketh his son or his daughter to pass through the fire* [any form of child sacrifice], *or that useth divination* [astrology, tarot, palm reading, etc.] *or an observer of times* [fortuneteller], *or an enchanter* [sorcerer], *or a witch, or a charmer, or a consulter with familiar spirits* [medium or channeler], *or a wizard, or a necromancer* [one who tries to contact, pray to, or inquire of the dead]. *For ALL that do these things are an ABOMINATION unto the LORD: and*

because of these abominations the LORD thy God doth drive them out from before thee. Thou shalt be perfect with the LORD thy God. For these nations, which thou shalt possess, hearkened unto observers of times and unto diviners: but as for thee [anyone who is in service to God], *the LORD thy God has not suffered thee so to do."*

Deut. 18:9-14

God calls this occult behavior an **ABOMINATION**. The next time you think about praying to a dead "saint", having your palm read, going to a psychic, doing yoga, or checking out your horoscope...remember that fact.

Though it is true some people consider the occult as total nonsense, the fact remains, according to the scripture passage you just read that God himself considers occultism not only authentic, but also dangerous.

The pentagram is just one of the symbols of sorcery which helps to generate and intensify this occult power.

We will now examine a few more examples of how the pentagram, which is without question an occult symbol used in the practice of magic, has affected the lives of those who have used it. The telltale results always lead down the same path: the path of *DARKNESS*.

Let's begin with one of the most popular rock bands in America.

MÖTLEY CRÜE

The history of Mötley Crüe is a rather long and involved one, so I will just touch on some highlights.

This group has been accused of being satanists, Devil worshipers, and the chosen sons of darkness and rebellion. This is exactly the public image they wanted to project when the group began.

Crüe guitarist Mick Mars told the interviewer on the "Eye on L.A." television show:

"What we do is what we're about, if it comes up demonic that's what we are."

Now you might be tempted to pass this off as typical rock star bravado, but Mick Mars is not the only one in the group who has ever underestimated the power of the demonic.

In *BAM* magazine July, 1982, bass player Nikki Sixx said:

"I've experienced witchcraft before and it doesn't intimidate me at all. It's nothing."

At one point in their career, Nikki also attempted to dissuade people from proclaiming their logo, the upside-down pentagram, was a demonic symbol associated with the occult. He told one interviewer, that having done a "study" of the pentagram, he uncovered no occultic connection with it at all, except information linking it with the mythical figure of the werewolf.

Well, Nikki may have thought little of the accusations leveled against the pentagram at that time, but he was soon to get a better education concerning its power, because the one on the wall of his apartment was already doing its job -- EVOKING DEMONS. Let me explain.

One day, Sixx and some of his friends were hanging around his apartment getting high, when all of a sudden a guitar pick that was lying on the table in front of them, flew into the air by itself and stuck into the ceiling. This supernatural demonstration was also accompanied by dishes moving around the apartment and the television changing channels by itself. This occult phenomenon experienced by Sixx and his friends is called POLTERGEIST ACTIVITY. The word "poltergeist" is a German word that means "noisy ghost". A poltergeist is recognized by many of those who study and investigate the supernatural as a mischievous spirit that specializes in moving objects. In one particular case in South America, a poltergeist was actually tearing stones out of a wall and hurling them at passing cars and pedestrians. Nikki Sixx, through his occult dabbling, had obviously attracted one or more of these spirits. He was receiving the wages due to him for touching the darkness: DEMONIC harassment. This, however, was only a very mild taste of the powers that he had attracted. Though early in his Rock & Roll career, a brash young Nikki Sixx thought nothing of dabbling with and even mocking these unseen powers, making foolish statements such as:

Heartbeat of the Dragon

Early Motley Crue promo shot. Nikki Sixx standing beneath band logo flag with the upside down pentagram. This was the picture on the inside album sleeve of their first record.

"We have skulls, PENTAGRAMS, and all kinds of satanic symbols on stage...I've always flirted with the Devil."[10]

He has recently learned the hard way it's not wise to flirt with the Devil.

A few years ago, Christmas season, 1987, he got a taste of what Satan's wrath is really all about. After a wild night of partying in the Devil's backyard, one of Nikki's "friends" decided to give him one shot for the road; not a drink, but a syringe filled with a potent dose of heroin. Sixx O.D.'d. Combined with all the other drugs and alcohol in his system, it proved to be a lethal dose. He fell unconscious to the floor and all his vital signs terminated. The ambulance was called and he was rushed to the hospital but it appeared to be too late. Nikki was pronounced D.O.A. by the doctors at Cedar-Sinai Medical Center in Los Angeles, California. Since Satan was clearly attempting to eliminate him and take him to Hell, it was only the compassion of a merciful God, and, according to Nikki, two needles full of adrenalin injected directly into his chest that were able to kickstart his heart and temporarily cheat the REAPER out of his motley prey (This is the incident that actually inspired the song title, "Kickstart My Heart", on their "Doctor Feelgood" album).

Nikki was radically shaken by his harrowing near-death experience, but did his dance with "Mr. D" teach him any lasting lessons? No...it didn't. Though his **"father who ain't in Heaven"** (as the Crüe sing on their hit, "Wild Side") unreservedly wanted to **KILL** him, Nikki Sixx has still chosen to remain the Dragon's loyal child...Some people **never learn.**

Was this the only tragedy that has ever struck Mötley Crüe? Not exactly. Tragedy struck even earlier in their career when Vince Neil, the band's lead singer, driving while intoxicated, caused a serious automobile accident. Neil survived the accident, but his passenger, Razzle, an acquaintance of the band and the drummer for the now defunct group Hanoi Rocks, was killed. Vince Neil sent his friend Razzle into a Christless eternity without any warning whatsoever. But once again, as with Nikki, by God's mercy, Vince also survived.

The members of Mötley Crüe spent many years wearing headbands with the inverted pentagram, their ungodly logo, placed directly in the *middle of their foreheads.* It was a perfect way to channel the demonic energy, which was focused on the pentagram, directly into their minds. This has obviously taken its toll.

Earlier in this chapter, we discussed the observations of Dr. A.S. Raleigh when he stated that the use of the upside-down pentagram would result in *INSANITY.* The songs of Mötley Crüe reflect *insanity* in full bloom.

Here is just a sample of their evil and violent lyrics from the album "Shout at the Devil":

"Out go the lights **in goes my knife**
Pull out his life
Consider that bastard dead"

BASTARD - MÖTLEY CRÜE

The lyrics for another song entitled "Too Young to Fall in Love" on the same album are even more reprehensible:

"Run for the hills
We're both sinners and saints

Not a woman, but a WHORE
I can just taste the HATE
Well, NOW I'M *KILLING* YOU
Watch your face TURNING BLUE"

Lyrics such as these are obviously inspired by a spirit of both **MURDER** and **DEATH.**
Guitarist, Mick Mars (Mars is the Roman god of war) also graced this same album with an instrumental composition which ends with someone singing, "God bless the **CHILDREN OF THE BEAST".**
The album even begins with a man reciting a narrative which includes a quote from one of the most infamous figures in history. The voice says, "Those who have the youth have the future". Who originally made this statement?...ADOLF HITLER!
There is, however, something very special about the album cover which houses this dark slab of vinyl. On the front of the album jacket, as well as the inside sleeve, is the inverted pentagram.
A later album entitled, "Girls Girls Girls", expresses even more lyrical violence. Here are some lyrics from one of the songs:

"The blade of my knife
Faced away from your heart
Those last few nights
It turned and **sliced you apart--**
I loved you so I set you free
I had to take your life--
KILLING YOU HELPED ME KEEP YOU HOME"
YOU'RE ALL I NEED - MÖTLEY CRÜE

The cover of their 5th album, "Doctor Feelgood", displays demonic and shamanic imagery. Skulls, bones, and a red-eyed demon head on the hilt of an athame (a ceremonial knife used in the performance of sorcery and magic) are just some of the occult images portrayed on the album cover.
The album itself is filled with songs about perverted sex: sex between two women (lesbianism), group sex with a prostitute, sadomasochistic sex with an

A recent Motley Crue album cover with shamanic and satanic symbols displayed.

under-aged school girl, as well as a song called "Rattlesnake Shake", whose graphic lyrics leave very little to the imagination, with lines like:

> "Sexy motion, just take my time
> The way she moves her lips
> Up and down my spine
> Got the rattle
> Snake wants to spit
> Call 9-7-6 and let my hand do the rest"

Nikki Sixx, the main lyricist for the group, describes this fantasy woman in his song as a "VOODOO CHILD...with a viper's smile" -- another lyric that evokes images of the occult.

Though the use of alcohol and illicit drugs (purely for reasons of self-preservation) has now been eradicated from the lives of the members of Mötley Crüe, their perverted sexual appetites (some of which are too offensive and detestable to mention) have more than compensated for the vacancy. Keep in mind, sexual sin is a major component of the celebration of satanism and witchcraft.

The Crue pose in their straight jackets

Murder, one definite aspect of insanity, is not only expressed in the lyrics of Nikki Sixx, but in his heart as well. In a recent interview with *Rip*, he relates his mental condition just before his trip to the hospital in 1987. He remembers:

> " I swear to God, I could have committed **murder** at that time in my life. I used to carry a blade around all the time, and I remember when we were recording some stuff at the studio, there was this styrofoam thing. I kept sticking the blade into this styrofoam thing, and someone went, 'What are you doing, man?' I go, 'Listen, pfft, pfft, pfft, the human body. **Wouldn't you just once like to FEEL A KNIFE GO INTO SOMEBODY'S BODY?** You only live once.'"[11]

If you are a Mötley Crüe fan, you just might want to go back and read that last quote again! In the mind of bassist Nikki Sixx, murder is not just a topic used in his lyrics. Perpetrating this heinous satanic act is something he has seriously contemplated. The spirit of murder obviously also resides in his heart.

There is a strange irony in the fact that some of the latest publicity pictures of Mötley Crüe show them dressed in *strait jackets*. If the space permitted, many more idiosyncrasies in the lives of the individual group members could be revealed , but I think by now you can see some of the results that using the pentagram has produced in the minds, hearts, and spirits of the Crüe boys...especially Nikki. Obviously, Dr. Raleigh's evaluation of the insanity producing effects of implementing the reverse pentagram has been more than validated.

But another group was using this symbol even earlier in rock history. The original name of the group was "Sister", a shock rock, black magic oriented band who used the pentagram in their logo long before pentagrams became popular paraphernalia for rockers. You say you never heard of "Sister"? Well maybe you would be a little more familiar with their present embodiment: W.A.S.P.!

W.A.S.P. - WE ARE SEXUAL PERVERTS

If you look on the inside vinyl band of their debut record just outside the label you will see the words, "We Are Sexual Perverts", scratched into the vinyl. Now whether the enigmatic initials that comprise their name, W.A.S.P., stand for, "We Are Sexual Perverts", "We Are Satan's People", or possibly something like, "We Ate Santa's Pajamas", no one really knows -- and since they prefer to keep everyone guessing, they're not telling.

Some members of W.A.S.P., however, in the past have associated themselves with the pentagram, and once again you can trace its legacy of insanity in their music. Incorporated into the music, lyrics, and earlier stage production of this group are images of violence and diabolism. One of the songs on their first album is a prime example. It says:

"I am a sinner, I kiss the breast
I am a sadist that RIPS THE FLESH
I take the women, curse those who enter
I am a killer and tormentor"

TORMENTOR - W.A.S.P.

Group leader Blackie Lawless (a revealing name in itself), is just another example of a rock performer, whether he is aware of it or not, who conceived an outrageous stage show based on tantric demonic mysticism and energized by the pentagram. But what about his own *verifiable* occult involvement? He told *Hit Parader* magazine in 1985 that he has "dabbled in the arts of witchcraft", but he also adds, "it's all bull". In an interview with *Circus* magazine, he related:

> "I studied the occult for about three years, it must have been about seven years ago, and I determined that it's a load of crap. I don't believe in it."

Blackie Lawless may not believe that using the pentagram and experimenting in the occult has had any effect on him, but the spirits of darkness that are attached to these things don't really care what he believes. Walk into *THEIR* territory and *your life is fair game*.

One very interesting action incorporated into the early W.A.S.P. stage shows was drinking blood from a skull. One wonders if Mr. Lawless knows that drinking wine or blood from a skull is pure black tantra still practiced in the back hills of India today.

Another part of their show was pretending to slit the throat of a half-naked woman tied up to a torture rack...A mock **HUMAN SACRIFICE**. Murder, torture, and human sacrifice, if you remember from an earlier chapter, are very tantric as well.

It is obvious that the magic of the pentagram has reached more deeply into the souls of Blackie Lawless and his group than even *he* realizes.

DANZIG

Another person we mentioned earlier to use and be adversely affected by the pentagram is Glenn Danzig.

His first band called the Misfits played thrash punk music. The group members wore a peculiar hairstyle, pulling all their hair down between their eyes in the middle of their foreheads. This radical coiffure had a name. They called it DEVILOCKS.

On the back of their "Earth A.D." album cover is the statement, "On Earth as it is in Hell". The front cover of this same album is filled with images of rotting,

Upper left: Crucified Glenn Danzig appears in goats head mask for "Home Video". Top upper right: Danzig stands in center of pentagram. Bottom upper right: Glenn Danzig standing before altar of satanic sacrifice. Both scenes taken from Danzig's "Home Video" of song "Mother". Below: Glenn poses for inside sleeve liner for second recording "Lucifuge". The Biblical quote of Jesus taken from the Gospel of John seen here is definitely apropos. The lusts of Glenn's father he is surely doing.

demonic looking creatures. Also on the back cover, an upside-down star (pentagram) is proudly displayed.

The second manifestation of the Misfits, after their break- up and subsequent reformation, was the group "Samhain", the name originally given to the satanic pagan holiday which Americans now celebrate as Halloween.

The Samhain celebration was an annual ritual held on October 31. On this night the Celtic Druid priests would travel the English countryside collecting frightened young peasant children to be used as human sacrifices to the Druid god Cerunnos, the HORNED HUNTER, also known as Kernos. On this night the English countryside was bathed in human blood.

This was the inspiration for the name of Danzig's second band. The music of Samhain was very similar to that of the Misfits with Glenn screaming out such songs as: "All Murder-All Guts-All Fun", "Black Dream", and "He-Who-Cannot-Be-Named". One of their albums entitled, "Unholy Passion", has a cover that depicts the group standing in front of a naked female form with a demon's head and wings. The title of the album clearly interprets what the picture is meant to visually represent. This title and picture of "Unholy Passion" is a definite reference to having sex with a SUCCUBUS, the feminine demon spirit previously mentioned in chapter two. This album contains songs with titles such as: "Unholy Passion," "Moribund", "All Hell", and "am i Misery". Eventually Samhain also disbanded.

The latest incarnation of these morbid rockers is the group simply known by the name of its leader, Danzig. Let's pause for just a moment to learn a little more about this group and its leader.

Nearly every band in existence markets T-shirts emblazoned with their band name and/or logo for the purpose of promotion. The artwork for one of the latest Danzig T-shirts, personally designed by Glenn himself, is purely Dragon inspired. In an excerpt from their first video release the group calls their "Home Video" is a candid conversation with Glenn Danzig concerning his personal spiritual beliefs, as well as how these beliefs have visually been expressed on the group's newest promotional T-shirt. Here is a transcript of a section of the interview:

Interviewer: Do you believe in God?

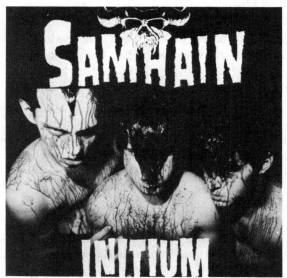

Above: Front cover of Samhain album "Initium" showing blood spattered group members sporting their devilock hairstyles.
Below: Samhain album "Unholy Passion" insinuating having sex with a succubus, female impersonating demon spirit

Glenn Danzig: Do I believe in God? Yeah...I believe in God. I don't believe in God as a...some old guy with a beard, but...as a power, yeah.

Int: What about Satan?

GD: Yeah. If you believe in God you believe in Satan. Uh...That doesn't necessarily mean you worship Satan, but yeah--Satan's probably one of the most misunderstood characters in the Bible or in Christian religion...God's most beloved angel. His original right-hand man.

Int: Who designed your new T-shirt?

GD: Uh...you mean the one with the demon--uh..the beastie guy strangling JESUS--His heart's glowin' and blood's comin' out of His eyes?

Int: That's the one.

GD: Yeah..I thought up that one.

Int: Do you think that's too much for some people?

GD: Yeah, it's cool.

Int: Don't you care?

GD: Yeah...I care, I like it. That's how much I care about it. I care about it so much that I had it put on a T- shirt. (Danzig laughs)

Int: Do you come under fire from any religious groups or organizations?

GD: Well, I haven't really got that much flack about it yet, but if they wanna fight and stop me...I probably know more about organized religion than they do...probably know more about their history and what they should be all about than they do. So, if they wanna fight...Come on!

Well, Glenn, or anybody else for that matter, I would gladly welcome the opportunity to meet with and debate you anywhere and anytime concerning the true origin and meaning of the Christian faith, God, and religion. God willing, I will get this opportunity.

Danzig's "Home Video", as they call it, ends with the song "Mother" from their first album. This excerpt opens with a quote from a famous Christian allegory called "Pilgrims Progress" written by John Bunyan. The quote they chose to use obviously taken out of proper context says, "Then I saw there was a way to Hell even from the gates of Heaven". The video then moves in for a close-up of Glenn Danzig singing:

"Mother
Tell your children not to walk my way
Tell your children not to hear my words
What they mean
What they say
Mother"

His singing voice, which sounds remarkably like that of the late Jim Morrison, then goes on to sing lyrics which undoubtedly are inspired by the same dark spirits who used, abused, and finally destroyed Morrison. Danzig sings:

"Father
Gonna take your daughter out tonight
Gonna show her my world
Oh, father
Not about to SEE YOUR LIGHT
But if you want to find HELL WITH ME
I can show you WHAT IT'S LIKE
'Til your BLEEDING"

SONG - MOTHER

Another song on the same album blatantly proclaims the true darkness behind this band. Their song, "Evil Thing", seems to be screaming out a deep despair from a man controlled and obsessed with evil. Danzig once again sings:

125

"When you look my way
See the emptiness in my eyes
And the evil thing
THAT I BRING
Soulless light--
In the dead of night
Let the DARKNESS RISE AGAIN"

This song then ends with what sounds almost like a plea from the demon in control of Danzig. He sings:

"Want the needing
Want to feel you near
Want your
Need your
LIFE
FEED IT TO ME!"

Their second recording entitled, "Danzig II-LUCIFUGE", is more of the same. It contains songs such as: "Long Way Back From Hell", "Her Black Wings", "Blood and Tears", "Devil's Plaything", as well as one more song openly and boldly proclaiming Glenn Danzig's total contempt for Jesus Christ. In this song entitled, "Snakes of Christ", we find Danzig singing:

"SERPENT JESUS
SNAKE OF CHRIST
NAILED TO A CROSS
OF A HOLY DESIGN
BLOOD TO WATER
WATER TO WINE
WHIP THE SOUL 'TIL A MOTHER CRIES
BRING IT DOWN
PIERCE THE SIDE
START THE *LEGEND* WITH A FUNERAL RITE
SERPENT JESUS
SNAKE OF CHRIST
GONNA BUILD YOU
A WORLD OF LIES"

It is very apparent by these lyrics that Danzig does not believe the biblical account of the life, crucifixion, and resurrection of the Son of God. However, to be totally fair, it is also important to note that Glenn's concepts of Christ were mainly inspired by reading esoteric, non-biblical accounts of the life of Jesus: In particular, the accounts related in The Lost Books of the Bible, which being pure fabrication are nonetheless believed by many deceived individuals: one of which is obviously Mr. Danzig.

It should now be quite evident by the information that you have just read concerning the life and musical career of Glenn Danzig, the pentagram has clearly raped, tortured, and is now in the process of destroying the soul of one more spiritually deceived "MISFIT".

The examples we have seen so far have been of the inverted pentagram. Now, let's take a look at a group who has turned it point up, just like they do in "white" witchcraft, and see if the story turns out any different.

RUSH

If you were to talk to any of the members of the group Rush and ask them if they were satanists, shamans, or witches, I'm sure you would receive a resounding...NO!!! But let's see some of the things this Canadian techno-rock band promotes and find out just where they are coming from.

On their album, "2112", you will notice the band logo. It is a *naked man* staring into a pentagram. It is interesting to note that many witches, besides using the pentagram in their rituals, also practice their "craft" *NAKED*, or what they call "SKYCLAD". They either draw the pentagram on the ground, sometimes even lying down inside it, or wear it in the form of an amulet, ring, or earring. It is a symbol which they firmly believe aids them in casting SPELLS.

Now you may be wondering why I'm drawing attention to the Rush logo which includes the naked man. Well, it's very simple. You see, if you remember in an earlier chapter, we mentioned Jesus meeting a demon possessed man in a graveyard (see Mark 5:1- 20). One point clearly made in this text is the fact that the possessed man he met was *NAKED*. It is interesting to note that once Jesus cast the demons out of this man he was immediately *clothed*. These

"Skyclad" witch draws "energy" from the forces of the pentagram by lying inside it while performing spells.

UNCLEAN SPIRITS inside the man were the ones who had caused him to go around naked. Here, in this Bible passage, there is obviously a direct correlation being drawn between public nudity and demonic activity.

Each year during certain religious festivals held in India in honor of Hindu deities and those who serve them, many yogis or "holy" men, who have made their bonds with the demonic spirit world through meditation and the emptying of their minds, come out and parade *NAKED* in the streets. These naked Hindu priests are considered to be the holiest gurus for a disciple to follow. Do you think there could be another correlation here between public nudity and the demonic? Since the demons on earth today are the same ones Jesus was personally casting out around 2000 years ago, I think you should know the answer to that one.

Now can you also see the correlation with the occult, Hinduism, and Rush's logo? The pentagram and nudity in direct association with each other, as in Rush's logo, can be linked, not only to witchcraft, but also with Hindu gurus and demonic possession. Interesting, isn't it?

Well, a logo displaying a naked man and a star is not exactly conclusive evidence in our case against Rush, so let's take a look at some of their music and determine what message they are trying to convey to their audience.

One of the songs on their "2112" album is entitled, "The Temple of Syrinx". Syrinx was the female demon companion of the god PAN. (Pan was one of the demon gods worshiped in the middle- eastern city of Caeserea Phillipi: the place where Jesus preached to his disciples about "the gates of hell" not ever prevailing against His church [Matt. 16:18].)

Pan, also, if you recall from an earlier chapter, was Aleister Crowley's favorite devil. He has always been a favorite of the ungodly.

Here are some words to the Rush song "2112" in which they sing of an allegiance to Syrinx:

"We are the priests of the temple of Syrinx
All the gates of life are held within our walls
Hold the RED STAR proudly high in hand"

What red star are they speaking of? The pentagram in their logo. It is a **red star**.

Side one of this "2112" album continues on, song after song, with its story of the power of music, and people from the stars coming back to earth to teach us how to live in peace and "wisdom". Residents of UFO's coming to teach us peace? Though I can truly relate to this theme because I had written many such songs myself, it is pure...New Age doctrine.

However, do not be surprised if, some day soon, UFO's actually do land and make contact. By the media attention given to the subject of flying saucers, and the entertainment worlds' continual promotion of these projected "close encounters", we have been sufficiently pre-programmed by movies such as, "The Day The Earth Stood Still", "E.T.", "Close Encounters of the Third Kind", "Mac And Me", and many others, to accept such encounters as beneficial probabilities. These UFO's, however, just like the others which have already been sighted all around the globe, will not be, as they may lead us to believe, intelligences from other worlds. They will be the same devils (fallen angels) that have occupied the space around the earth since man was banished from the Garden of Eden.

In another song from the "2112" album entitled, "Oracle: The Dream", are these words:

Above: Inside cover of Rush 2112 album showing their naked man/pentagram logo.

"I stand atop a **spiral stair**,..."

In New Age thought, the symbol of the spiral (which we will be discussing in a later chapter) is an extremely significant image. It can even be used to represent a "666" (the mark of the Beast -- Rev. 13:18).

"...An **oracle** confronts me there..."

Oracle in this sense is just another name for a **spirit guide** or **master of "wisdom"**. These masters are some of the more intelligent and powerful of the fallen angels.

"...He leads me on light years away
Through **ASTRAL** nights, galactic days"

Astral travel or projection is the ability for one's spirit to temporarily evacuate one's body and travel in the spirit realm. This power is given by high level demonic spirits to their followers. It is a practice that has been utilized by gurus and occultists for millennia.

Side one of this "2112" album ends with the main character in their song committing *SUICIDE.*

The first song on side two begins a new theme: ILLEGAL DRUGS. It trumpets the joys of a global journey in search of a better high. We travel along with Rush in their song called "A Passage to Bangkok" from the hemp fields of Colombia, to the jungles of Jamaica, to the heights of Acapulco, Mexico sampling the drugs that each location has made famous. Then it's on to the East, stopping in Bangkok, Thailand; Lebanon; Afghanistan; and Katmandu, Nepal. This entire song is about smoking marijuana, opium, and hashish. Each location mentioned in the song is well known for the potency and specific brand names of its illicit export drugs: Colombian buds, Jamaican ganja (used religiously by the Rastafarians and reggae musicians like Ziggy Marley, who sings the glories of pot in a song called "Urb-an Music" on his album entitled, "One Bright Day"), Acapulco Gold, Moroccan black hash, Thai sticks, Lebanese blond hash and hash oil, Afghanistan hash oil, and Katmandu hashish and opium. Here are the lyrics to this song:

"Our first stop is in Bogota
To check Colombian fields
The natives smile and pass along
A sample of their yield
Sweet Jamaican pipe dreams
Golden Acapulco nights
Then Morocco, and the East,
Fly by morning light

We're on the train to Bangkok
Aboard the Thailand Express
We'll hit the stops along the way
We only stop for the best

Wreathed in smoke in Lebanon
We burn the midnight oil
The fragrance of Afghanistan
Rewards a long days toil

Pulling into Katmandu
Smoke rings fill the air
Perfumed by a Nepal night
The Express gets you there"

The members of Rush are obviously very familiar with the most *POTENT* and spiritually damaging drugs in the world. And remember, once again these *ARE* the drugs used by gurus of India who are still leading many followers from the West into their Eastern mystical darkness.

The last song on side two completes the New Age teaching and indoctrination contained within this album. The final verses tell their "New Age" philosophy:

"What you own is *your* own kingdom
What you do is *your* own glory
What you love is *your* own power
What you live is *your* own story
In *your* head is the answer
Let it guide you along
Let *your* heart be the anchor
And the beat of *your* song"

The answer to life that Rush gives you, is found in the *self;* in *your own power*. Unfortunately, for them as well as anyone who might acquiesce to their advice, they are wrong. I looked for answers inside myself for many years, and I can assure you, you are not going to find Truth within the human psyche.

This New Age fantasy theme is continued throughout their next two musical offerings.

In 1977 came the album, "A Farewell To Kings", containing similar New Age ideas. On it they sing:

"Atomized - at the core
Or through the **ASTRAL** door
To soar..."
SONG - "CYGNUS X-1 BOOK 1 - THE VOYAGE"

Here once again is the reference to soaring during astral projection.

The next album to be released by the group in 1978 was entitled "Hemispheres". This album is also chock full of New Age imagery. On the album cover is a picture of a group of brains floating in the air. On the surface, the album title and the floating brains may not seem to mean much, but beneath the surface is where the message lies. What could this picture and album title be portraying? Let's find out.

Marilyn Ferguson, New Age author of The Aquarian Conspiracy (a book with a stylized "666" right on the cover), places a great emphasis on the power of the brain, and its link with the mind. She especially draws the distinction between the functions of the right and left sides of the brain called *hemispheres*. She also states there are certain techniques which we should engage in to "reopen the bridge" between the two sides of the brain. What does she suggest will help this process:

> "Meditation, chanting, and similar techniques increase the coherence and harmony in the brainwave patterns; they bring about greater synchrony between the HEMISPHERES..."[12]

Meditation, chanting, drug use, etc. is undoubtedly the spiritual path that Rush is hoping their fans will follow...

But it goes even deeper than that.

If you look very closely at the front of the album cover, you will see two men standing on a brain; one man on the right side, one on the left side. In New Age teaching, such as that purported by Marilyn Ferguson, the *right* side of the brain governs art, music, sensuality, and imagination. Standing on the *right* side of the brain on Rush's album cover is a naked man in a dance pose; a perfect representation of this concept. The *left* side of the brain, also according to New Age teaching, governs the more disciplined areas of our lives such as mathematics, knowledge, and organization. Standing on the *left* side of the brain on Rush's album cover is a man in a three piece business suit with a very austere look on his face. He obviously represents order, organization, and logic. Once again, this is a perfect correlation to this New Age understanding taught by Marilyn Ferguson.

As you can now clearly see, with the left brain/right brain concept, totally identifiable with the New Age movement, Rush has once again opened the door of New Age thought for their audience.

Above: The front cover of Rush "Hemispheres" visually depicting left brain / right brain New Age spiritual teaching.

Below: Front cover of the Aquarian Conspiracy by Marilyn Ferguson. Notice the stylized 666 in the cover design. This book is one of the "bibles" of the New Age Movement.

Many New Age leaders are also well known for their worship of pagan gods and goddesses, an act strictly forbidden in the Bible. Rush bass player and vocalist, Geddy Lee, sings on this same album about the gods Apollo and Dionysus and then proceeds to reinterpret the biblical meaning of Armageddon to be nothing more than a struggle between one's heart and one's mind; another New Age concept covered in Ferguson's book. As you can now see, there is a lot more to Rush's "Hemispheres" than meets the eye, ear, or...*brain*.

Though I cannot fault the clear desire portrayed in many of Rush's song lyrics for love to dominate our lives, this transition from hatred, violence, and destruction to brotherhood and love will not come about by merely uniting our hearts with our minds. Both of these components of man -- the human heart and the human mind, are born in the corruption of sin. The Bible states:

"The heart is deceitful above all things and desperately wicked: who can know it?"

Jeremiah 17:9

God *KNOWS* the depths of the human heart and understands us well.

Rush's New Age salvation theme continues from song to song, album to album; however, on the "Moving Pictures" album it takes an all too familiar turn. On this album they begin to manifest, just as in all the other groups we have already mentioned, who they *really* represent.

On the song, "Witch Hunt", lyricist Neil Peart pens some lines of clearly anti-Christian flavor, directed against people who refuse to apathetically tolerate movies and books that promote darkness and occult practices. Peart writes:

"Madmen fed on fear and lies
To beat and burn and kill
They say there are strangers who threaten us-
They say there is strangeness too dangerous
In our theaters and bookstore shelves
Those who know what's best for us-
Must rise and save us, from ourselves
Quick to judge
Quick to anger
Slow to understand

> Ignorance and prejudice and fear
> Go hand in hand"
>
> "WITCH HUNT" - RUSH

Who are these "madmen" that Rush is deriding? This song is clearly meant to be an attack on people who stand in opposition to the occult. *True* Christians who are trying to keep the Dragon's darkness from infecting all the people are quite often accused of being on a "witch hunt".

Now, some people *CHOOSE* to walk in darkness. That is their right. Many others, however, are just helpless pawns caught in the Dragon's deadly chess game; ignorant and naive victims being sucked into the power vortex of this new dark age of mystical delusion. *They* can still be reached. No one in this world NEEDS to be DEMONIZED or polluted in the name of artistic freedom of expression.

We are *ALL* entitled to freedom of expression, but we who truly understand this spiritual war in which we are now engaged, are by God's LOVE and mercy, also entitled to stand in the position of intercessors and informants for those who are already ensnared, or about to be snared, in Satan's occult/New Age web.

Am I finished with Rush yet? NOT QUITE.

Here is another rather intriguing fact concerning this group. The main lyricist of Rush is drummer Neil Peart. He credits one particular person with being the major source of his inspiration. The name of this "genius" is author and philosopher Ayn Rand. It is very interesting that the works of this woman Ayn Rand (another person who advocates looking into the *SELF* as the answer to humanity's problems) are also on the suggested reading list of another infamous organization. Who, you might ask? None other than Anton LaVey and the Church of SATAN! More coincidence?...Not likely. You see, in one way or another, *ALL* those who serve the Dragon, **whether they know it or not**, are *spiritually* linked together.

BLACK MAGIC

Now just in case I still haven't convinced you that the pentagram is a dangerous occult symbol, let's take one more look at someone who knew exactly what it *could* do and used it quite often. Care to venture a guess as to who it might be? If you guessed **Aleister Crowley**, you're right again.

This infamous man is largely responsible for the resurrection of the occult in our century. I have already given you a brief synopsis of his life, but our main concern now will be to see just how familiar he was with the occult symbol which is the focus of this chapter. I can give you one word to describe how familiar he was with the use of the pentagram... *VERY*. As you will now see, Mr. Crowley, in the performance of his black magick rituals, used the pentagram quite often and quite, I might add, effectively.

From his biography on Crowley, author Colin Wilson writes of one such ritual:

"The climax came...in an episode involving the sacrifice of a cat. The animal had scratched Crowley when he tried to throw it out of the room...He made the **sign of the pentagram** over it with his magic staff and ordered it to remain there until the hour of sacrifice. The cat did just that."[13]

With his magickal command, Crowley actually supernaturally controlled the behavior of this animal.

This "sacrifice" incident goes on, however, to include one more use for the pentagram. Wilson continues:

"Crowley dipped his finger in the blood [the unfortunate cat's] and **traced the pentagram on Loveday's forehead**."[14]

Raoul Loveday was Crowley's disciple, as well as one of his black magick apprentices. That is, until the day he died. (which, by the way, happened quite suddenly and on the exact day that Crowley had foretold that it would, just a few weeks before.)

Now, notice once again if you will, exactly where Crowley had drawn the cat's blood pentagram on his assistant Loveday...on his **forehead!** Where did Mötley Crüe and their followers wear their pentagrams? On their *FORE-HEADS!!!* Aleister Crowley knew why he was putting the pentagram on Raoul Loveday's forehead: He was practicing black magic. What about Mötley Crüe? Whether they know it or not, *so are they!*

Another of Crowley's magickal apprentices also used this powerful occult symbol. From his book entitled, The Black Arts, author Richard Cavendish recounts for us one of those incidents where the pentagram was once again used. He writes:

> "In 1909 Crowley and Victor Neuberg visited Algiers and went south into the desert. They decided to conjure up a 'mighty devil' called Chorozon. The magic circle was drawn in the sand and the triangle of Solomon from the LEGEMETON outside it."[15]

Crowley and his assistant were actually conjuring a devil in the desert. Their black magic worked. This is what happened next when Crowley allowed himself to be taken over and DEMON POSSESSED!:

> "Crowley wore a black robe with a hood which enveloped his head but had eyeslits. He crouched in the triangle to allow the demon to take POSSESSION of him...Suddenly there was a loud, wild laugh and Chorozon appeared visibly in the triangle."[16]

Then the scene changed again:

> "Chorozon who was now in the shape of Crowley but **naked,** begged for water to quench his thirst. Neuberg again refused, commanding the demon to obey him by THE NAMES OF GOD and by the **PENTAGRAM.**"[17]

Over and over again, the pentagram is mentioned in connection with Aleister Crowley. Was this occult symbol important to this black magician and his apprentices? You bet it was!

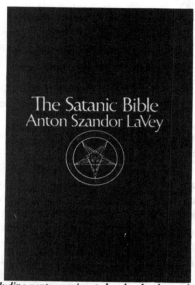

Cover of Satanic Bible including pentagram/goats head or baphomet logo. Notice the Hebrew characters between the inside and outside circles. These symbols spell the word "Leviathan", another Biblical name for Satan.

Ex-satanist high priest, Mike Warnke, also found occasion to use this symbol in his satanic black mass ceremonies. In his autobiographical book, The Satan Seller, he remembers one particular incident. He writes:

> "Now I will draw an **upside down star** on the [naked] girl's stomach with the freshly spilled blood. From the weird utterances that now came from her mouth I knew we were being graced by the presence of one of the denizens of hell."[18]

Many other satanists and black magicians still use this symbol in their black mass rituals and ceremonies. Even the official "Church of Satan" uses the inverted pentagram, complete with the goat's head inside the star (called a Baphomet), as their main occult symbol. It is also emblazoned on the cover of the Satanic Bible.

Have any other Rock & Roll musicians, besides the ones we have previously mentioned, found occasion to use this same symbol? Read on and see.

VENOM

Another group to use the pentagram symbol, including the goat's head inside the star, is a band by the name of Venom. Truly a name befitting their character.

They call their fans their **LEGIONS.** Interesting that they would use this particular term to describe their followers. Why do I find it so interesting? Let me explain.

As we have already mentioned, in the Bible is an account of a time when Jesus Christ was confronted by a demon possessed man. Jesus asked him, *"What is your name".* The demon who spoke through the man said, *"My name is LEGION for we are many"* (Mark 5:9). The demon leader within the man called himself Legion. Another interesting correlation.

If you asked the members of Venom about their satanic beliefs they would probably laugh and tell you that it's only a show business gimmick, but if you take a closer look at their songs you will once again see for yourself the insanity of the pentagram reigning supreme.

Let's take a look at some of the lyrics on their "At War With Satan" album and you will understand just what I mean. Here is just a quick example:

> "Damnation has sunk it's talons deep into the womb of utopia spilling forth great streams of virginal purity and bliss. The golden throne of tetragrammaton is ablaze. **His majesty** sits proud, the joyous drones of celebrations enact scenes of blasphemy, lust and destruction **RAPING THE HOLY TRINITY."**

When Venom sings about "His majesty", they are *not* referring to God. They are referring to *SATAN*.

There are many more bands who also use this symbol. Time and time again, the EVIL story remains the same.

The lyrical content of their songs comes straight from the PIT. Over and over and over again, their lyrics spew out blasphemy, murder, and perversion. Here are a few more examples of groups who employ the pentagram. Without question, these will emphasize my point:

GROUP NAME: Onslaught
SONG TITLE: Fight With the Beast

> "Demons of hell bear the mark of the Beast
> The sons of the Dragon are born
> Summoned to earth Armageddon is here
> **To slaughter the Christian hordes**
> Destroying the temples Jehova has lost
> The **NAZARENE WILL FESTER IN HELL!!!**"

GROUP NAME: Slayer
SONG TITLE: Jesus Saves

> "You go to church you kiss the cross
> You will be saved at any cost
> You have your own reality
> Christianity
> **JESUS SAVES**, listen to you pray
> You think you'll see the pearly gates
> When death takes you away

GROUP NAME: Celtic Frost (formerly Hellhammer)
SONG TITLE: Dawn of Megiddo

> "Humiliated in human form
> We have to die to be reborn
> Awaiting the final judgment
> The dawn now lifts
> Subjects of flesh slaves of lust
> The **CROSS HAS FAILED** (you won't see)
> The coming FALL"

GROUP NAME: SUICIDAL TENDENCIES

SONG TITLE: SUICIDAL MANIAC

"A birth that came from more than sound
Now rages on from town to town
A giant grows more every day
And now the Maniac is here to stay

A feeling you can't kill
It's the power, it's a will
Controls your thoughts but you can't see--
A power of another kind
A PRESENCE that is growing out of SOUND

And now it's come, the time the Maniac I'll meet
He takes my hand and now I bow down to his feet
His love for me is like a FATHER TO A SON
And now the **Maniac and I are ONE**

I bow to his might
Too powerful to fight
It's my destiny
Now the Maniac **LIVES INSIDE OF ME**"

Suicidal Tendencies has just given us another lyrical Rock & Roll story of demonic POSSESSION.

Can you sense the true *INSANITY* in all these lyrics? The pentagram has clearly taken its toll on the minds, hearts, and spirits of *ALL* those who have enlisted it's service.

I think by now, you should be able to see that the pentagram, whether pointed up or down, is much more than just a decoration or an interesting geometrical configuration. To the forces of darkness who created it, it is a true symbol of allegiance to be used by their followers. It is, in fact, a catalyst for developing a spiritual bond with fallen angels; a doorway if you will, allowing them entry in and out of the infernal spiritual dimension of HADES.

Why would we find the pentagram on the cover of the <u>Satanic Bible?</u> Very simple...It is **THE DEVIL'S STAR**.

TWINKLE TWINKLE EVIL STAR: THE LEGACY OF THE PENTAGRAM

Top left: Onslaught. Top right: Slayer. Bottom left: Celtic Frost. Bottom right: Venom. Examples of pentagrams on various album covers. The music on these recordings, as well as the groups are truly "blessed" by the dragon.

CHAPTER 11

OUT OF THE MOUTH OF THE DRAGON

"and I saw three unclean spirits like frogs come OUT OF THE MOUTH OF THE DRAGON and out of the mouth of the beast and out of the mouth of the false prophet"

Revelation 16:13

"and there was given unto him [anti-Christ] a mouth speaking great things and blasphemies...and he opened his mouth in BLAS-PHEMY against God to BLASPHEME His Name and His Tabernacle and them that dwell in Heaven"

Revelation 13:5,6

In case you haven't guessed it by now, the Dragon HATES JESUS CHRIST, the *TRUE* GOD, and HIS *TRUE* CHURCH. This is a fact made even more unequivocal when you consider the scriptures that you just read taken from the Book of Revelation.

During his powerful but brief tribulational reign as god over this world system, the Beast or anti-Christ will be very well known for his *BLASPHEMY* against the LIVING God. It will be his trademark.

Many of these modern day shamans, the high priests and priestesses of Rock & Roll, have willingly accepted this trademark as their own. Their mouths are filled with the same blasphemous Dragon's breath; their words full of searing verbal *fire* directed against The MOST HIGH GOD. Whether in their songs or in their interviews, they have learned well to speak their father's mind. Here are just a few examples of what the Dragon's offspring have taught their disciples about God, Jesus, Christianity, and religion.

145

JEFFERSON AIRPLANE

Just recently many music groups of the past who had disbanded have decided to reunite: The Rolling Stones, The Doobie Brothers, Poco, the Allman Brothers Band, Lynyrd Skynyrd, and even the well scattered and broken fuselage of the Jefferson Airplane (JA) has decided to come together for one more flight.

The Airplane has always had an infamous reputation for their promotion of rebellion against authority, as well as for their open drug consumption and abuse; but they also spent a lot of time walking that old familiar highway of Rock & Roll land called Blasphemy Blvd.

In the past, JA lead singer Grace Slick was rather proud to be known as blasphemer extraordinaire. To show her true contempt for Christianity she named her illegitimate child "god", saying it would be spelled with a small "g" because Slick quipped, "we have to be humble about this". As we are about to see, however, the Jefferson Airplane took their blasphemous mockery of God right out of their hearts and injected it right into their music.

On one of their albums entitled, "Long John Silver", is a song called, "The Son of Jesus", which is a perfect example of a deep hatred for both God and His Word. The song lyrically depicts the very same type of sin-cursed and mentally disturbed Jesus portrayed in the movie released in the summer of 1988 called, "The Last Temptation of Christ". In both instances, the movie and this song, Jesus is depicted as a lustful and confused man who ends up fathering a child by Mary Magdalene, and in both cases, the issue of the accuracy of the biblical account of Christ's life is viciously attacked, ridiculed, and questioned. But Grace Slick and the Jefferson Airplane had launched *their* attack clear back in *1972!*

Here are some of the lyrics to this sacreligious song written by Paul Kantner of the Jefferson Airplane:

"Jesus had a son by Mary Magdalene
And he rode the land like the man
Who went before
Young Jesus raised him loud
Mother Mary raised him proud

And he tracked the men who laid his father down
One day the Pilate died with the fire in his side
Herod did die too
Not the way he wanted to
Y'see the **child knew the secrets of Egypt**
And Isis"

    The beginning of this verse is self-explanatory, but for those not well versed in ancient Egyptian mythology, I will explain the last line.

    The last half of the verse you just read not only intimates that Jesus Christ never rose from the dead, but it also implies that Pontius Pilate and King Herod, who were primarily responsible for the crucifixion of Jesus Christ, both died from curses which were placed on them by the *SON* of Jesus who used the ancient black magic of the Egyptian goddess Isis to do the work. That is exactly what these lyrics mean. However, they go on to say:

"So you think young Jesus Christ never smiled
At a lady
And you think young Mary never saw him
Smile wild and free
YOU WON'T READ IT IN THE BIBLE
BUT IF YOU LOOK YOU'RE LIABLE
TO COME ACROSS THE *TRUTH* ABOUT THE
MAN FROM GALILEE"

    The song says more, but I think you get the picture. Lyrics such as these show at least *ONE* thing. The members of the Jefferson Airplane have no idea whatsoever about the "truth" concerning the "Man from Galilee". But there is one part of this song that is totally accurate; the line which says, "You won't read it in the Bible". Truer words were never spoken. You definitely won't read these Dragon-inspired lies about Jesus Christ in the Bible.

JANE'S ADDICTION - JA OF THE 90's

Though Grace Slick and her band, the Jefferson Airplane, JA for short, were quite infamous in their day for their blasphemy and rebellion, they are even now

Shaman of the 1990's Perry Farrell of Jane's Addiction, complete with his tambourine or drum type instrument.

being surpassed by the revolutionary Rock & Roll shamans of the present; one of whom is Perry Farrell, lead vocalist for the group Jane's Addiction.

Aside from his preoccupation with sexual perversion evidenced by his artwork (seen on their album covers), and expressed in his music and videos (songs with themes such as stealing and urinating on himself in the shower), Farrell originally adopted a highly unusual appearance which could easily place him in the category of shaman in the truest sense of the word. To understand this fact even more clearly, one needs only to watch his frenzied trance-state dance of possession when he is performing on stage with his group.

The reason I'm giving this special attention to Jane's Addiction is because of a personal observation: Just as the Jefferson Airplane, the JA of the past were the Rock & Roll revolutionaries of their time; the new JA, Jane's Addiction, are without question the Dragon's trend setting Rock & Roll revolutionaries of today. I assert that both these groups reside in the same **darkness**. But lest we

Front cover of second album by Jane's Addiction. The album title says it all "Ritual de lo Habitual". Notice the doll figures and other items in the picture. These are fetishes used in the rituals of Santeria.

judge too quickly, let's find out a little more information about the lead vocalist of the new JA.

Perry Farrell, true to the generally accepted pattern of modern day morality, was living with his girlfriend, Casey, for about five years. Not long ago, however, he decided that it was about time to tie the knot. They would be married. Now, on the surface that sounds commendable, but don't be too hasty in your congratulations for his act of moral conformity. Perry Farrell, by his own evaluation, has been a rebel all of his life; so do you think this future connubial union would take on any other characteristics than those of a rebel? As a quite well known quip so accurately states, "not a snowball's chance in Hell". Oh, he definitely planned on getting married, but the real issue stems from the fact of where the ceremony would be held and who would perform it. That is the part that draws my interest. To get the details of the then future wedding ceremony, let's let Perry tell us himself as he explained it to *SPIN* magazine September, 1990. He said: "...I'm just going to take her down to Mexico and marry her. But it's going to be by SANTERIAN BRUJOS." ...And that is exactly what he did.

What, you may ask, is a Santerian Brujo? That is a question easily answered.

SANTERIA, a word literally translated "worship of saints", is a pagan religion of South America which, as many of the other South American pagan religions, blends the blood sacrifice and possession of African and Haitian Voodoo with a strong dose of Roman Catholic idol worship. It has worked it's way into the United States via the immigrants of Mexico and Cuba.

A *BRUJO* is a **black magic sorcerer**. So a Santerian Brujo is a **Voodoo sorcerer**. That is the minister that Perry Farrell had officiating at his wedding.

Their second major album, "Ritual de lo Habitual", has a cover loaded with images of fetishes used in the practice of Santeria which they also use on stage when they perform live.

The members of Jane's Addiction apparently don't mind courting darkness in their lives *OR* their music. Bassist, Eric Avery, is well aware of the underlying spirit behind it. He told *SPIN* in the same interview mentioned earlier, "There's a gray area like **darkness** to our music that is intangible".

Though their musical "darkness" seems to be somewhat of an enigma to Avery, if he would just inquire of their revolutionary forefathers, The Jefferson Airplane, this mystery could easily be solved. The Airplane obviously employed these same dark powers. The telltale signs of this influence consistently show up in their music. How I can be so sure of this evaluation is something you are about to discover. The spirit inspiring the words for the songs of Jane's Addiction is once again, as with the Airplane, the same Christ hating spirit. In the songs of Jane's Addiction, as well as those of the old JA, is the exact same blasphemy against God. The similarity in the lyrical content of both groups, specifically the blasphemous attack against Jesus, is rather uncanny. Though they are separated by some 20 years, amazingly enough one of the subjects Perry Farrell chooses to sing about is, once again, the alleged sexual relations between Jesus and Mary Magdalene. But this time it's *two* Mary's instead of just one. Here are some of the lyrics written by Perry Farrell, from the Jane's Addiction song, "Three Days":

> *"EROTIC JESUS* lays with his Mary's
> Loves his Marys
> Loves his Marys

Bits of puzzle fitting together"

Though I am well aware of the fact that Farrell means these lyrics in his song to be an autobiographical symbolism of his love life, the words you have just read, in the cases of both groups, could justifiably be called nothing less than a satanic attack against the character of God, a HOLY and SINLESS Savior. Whether from the old JA or the new one, they are truly straight from the Dragon's heart.

But as you are about to discover, many more of yesterday's, as well as today's, Rock & Roll heroes mirror this same anti- Christian mind-set.

Here are just a few more of the hundreds of examples I *could* have used.

THE YOUNG DRAGONS SPEAK

SPIN magazine interview with group Duran Duran:
SPIN: Which event in history would Duran Duran most like to have witnessed?

DURAN DURAN: We would have loved to have been at Woodstock, **even more than the parting of the Red Sea or THE CRUCIFIXION![1]**
JOHN TAYLOR - DURAN DURAN

"That Judeo-Christian story that we've been living for 2,000 years, is that God and everything is some other thing outside of ourselves -- that continual us-and- them relationship with God, with children, with nature, the environment where we've conquered nature, worshiped God, we deal with children, its this separation business that *I DON'T BELIEVE EXISTS.*"[2]
JOHN LENNON

"When I was growing up, I was religious in a passionate, adolescent way. Jesus Christ was like a MOVIE STAR, MY FAVORITE IDOL OF ALL."[3]

MADONNA

"You find God and you find yourself. I think **God is inside everybody.**"[4]

"When I talk about God I don't mean some *DUDE* in a CAPE AND BEARD COMING DOWN TO EARTH. To me, he's *IN EVERYTHING* if you look at it that way."[5]

PRINCE

"Donnie is studying Islam and Christianity and Buddhism but believes *ALL RELIGIONS ARE GOOD* because they strengthen and better the followers of its faith."[6]

DONNIE WAHLBERG - NEW KIDS ON THE BLOCK

This religious evaluation by Donnie (idol of screaming young girls worldwide) Wahlberg is dead **WRONG.** *ALL* religions are *NOT* good! Buddhism, one of the ones he is studying, preaches reincarnation and promotes meditation, two anti-Christian teachings.

On the other hand, if a person happens to convert *TO* Christianity *FROM* Islam (the other religion he says he is studying), in many Moslem controlled countries, the family or acquaintances of that person might *KILL HIM*. The simple fact is that fanatical Moslems are responsible for killing, raping, and torturing Christians and burning or blowing up over 200 Christian churches in Africa alone. **NO DONNIE...all religions are NOT GOOD!**

"We don't believe in the Devil - **but none of us believes in God either.** We view both of them the same way - as creations by man to hold power over other men. They're just ancient beliefs that people are scared to stop believing in. The time for religion has passed."[7]

TOM G. WARRIOR - CELTIC FROST

"God is *MAN MADE*. We invented this [concept of God] to keep other members of mankind and especially womankind under control. It's a protectionist racket."[8]

ANDY PARTRIDGE - XTC

"Rock music is a greater influence over the souls of men than **primitive Christianity.**"[9]

JOHN DENVER

"If Jesus Christ came back and took me for a beer I'd never change. I mean he was one hell of a strange boy himself."[10]

TRANSVESTITE SINGER - WAYNE/JAYNE COUNTY

"I don't believe in Jesus Christ."[11]

OZZY OSBOURNE

"I'd like to say that organized Christianity has done more harm than any other single force I can think of in the world."[12]

LEON RUSSELL

"If God is such hot stuff, why is he afraid to have other gods before him?...I guess I always wanted **to BE GOD.**"[13]

GENE SIMMONS - KISS

"If Jesus had been indicted in a modern court he would have been examined by a doctor, found to be obsessed by a delusion, declared incompetent and incapable of pleading his case and **sent to an asylum.**"[14]

MICK JAGGER - ROLLING STONES

"There is much more validity to Hinduism than anything in Christianity."[15]
I couldn't relate to Christ being the only Son of God."[16]

GEORGE HARRISON - THE BEATLES

"If Jesus Christ came back now, He'd have to come back as a twat (very derogatory slang term for a woman). To come back as he was would be too preposterous for this age."[17]

JULIAN COPE

"I'm of this generation that has no religion. We have found something **finer than Christianity**."[18]

DONOVAN

"The night life balances my scheme of things. I love watching the sun come up while you're coming in. It's like **God** SALUTING ME for having an evening that would do him proud."[19]

DAVID LEE ROTH

"...if I have a religion, it's the religion of the self. I don't follow anybody."[20]

DARYL HALL - HALL & OATES

"...I certainly don't believe in an *OLD BEARDED MAN* up there. I see God as **A FORCE** that guides and unites our finest actions and sensibilities. We might call **IT** God because we have no other way of explaining it."[21]

DAVID BYRNE - TALKING HEADS

"I can remember as a kid praying to God -- you say a little prayer to this *WHITE MAN IN THE SKY* **WITH A BEARD** -- and not being satisfied, because that wasn't how God felt to me. When I pray now, I'm praying to a kind of **ENERGY**."[22]

NENEH CHERRY

"I make music for the **glory of God** and the recreation of the mind and body."[23]

DAVID COVERDALE - WHITESNAKE

Whoa!! Wait a minute! Did David Coverdale, lead singer for the band Whitesnake, say he makes his music for the glory of God? Let's take a look at some of his latest lyrics:

SONG - Cheap an' Nasty

You're fully loaded with cruise control
My four wheels rock with your backseat roll
You're cheap an' nasty
All you want to do is give it up
Cheap an' nasty
Come on and do the dirty with me

ALBUM - SLIP OF THE TONGUE

I guess those lyrics are for the glory of god. The god of lust, fornication, and illicit sex: Satan, the "god of this world [system]".

THE DRAGON'S KIDS SING TOO

The previous quotes were just a few examples of blasphemy and anti-Christ fervor; but if you really want to know what musicians believe or disbelieve, just read their songs. Most musicians actually choose communicating their beliefs through their music, as opposed to talking about them. In this regard let's see if 'the song remains the same'.

Here are some of the lyrics to songs written and recorded by some of the most popular and well known musicians and singers Rock & Roll has ever known, from the past *and* present, that will clearly prove my point.

I will begin with one of the more tragic examples. I say tragic because it was a poem which was later to become a song: a poem written by Aquarian voodoo child Jimi Hendrix just hours before he died. Can you believe he spent his last moments thinking about Jesus? Well, in fact he did. But as is the case in much of the Devil's ongoing misinformation campaign against Christ, Jimi was contemplating the **WRONG JESUS**. Had he been thinking about the Jesus who had died for his sins, the ETERNAL GOD of Heaven and Earth, who could forgive him and give him everlasting peace, joy, and **SALVATION**, he may not have had to make that unimaginable and terrifying trip that he was to undergo just a few hours later; a trip into the bowels of endless despair and hopelessness; a one way journey into the netherworld of HADES from which he would **NEVER RETURN**. Yes, had he been thinking about the loving, forgiving,

saving Jesus, that horrendous journey may never have taken place -- but......he
was not. The Jesus that Jimi was contemplating was this one:

> The story of Jesus
> so easy to explain
> after they crucified him,
> a woman, she claimed his name
> The story of Jesus
> the whole Bible knows
> went all across the Desert
> and in the middle, he found a rose
> There should be no questions
> there should be no lies
> *HE WAS MARRIED EVER*
> happily after
> for all the Tears we cry

JIMI HENDRIX

Hendrix was just one of many who have maligned the Lord Jesus Christ and
His doctrine. Unfortunately he never got a chance to correct his mistake. The
following songs are more examples by others who have done the same:

SONG - The Oath

"...I DENY JESUS CHRIST THE *DECEIVER*
And I abjure the Christian faith
Holding in contempt all of its works..."

KING DIAMOND & MERCYFUL FATE
ALBUM - DON'T BREAK THE OATH

SONG - Soft Parade

"When I was back there in seminary school there was a person
there who put forth the proposition that you can petition the Lord
with prayer. Petition the Lord with prayer. Petition the Lord with

prayer. You *CANNOT* PETITION THE LORD WITH PRAYER."

JIM MORRISON/THE DOORS
ALBUM - SOFT PARADE

SONG - Hallowed Be My Name

"It would be nice
To walk upon the water
Talk again to angels
At my side
I just came back to show you
All my words are golden
So have no gods before me
I'M THE *LIGHT*"

ALICE COOPER
ALBUM - LOVE IT TO DEATH

SONG - Fight With The Beast

"...Replacing the cross with the mark of the beast
The kingdoms of Jesu have fell..."

NIGE ROCKETT - ONSLAUGHT
ALBUM - THE FORCE

SONG - HYMN 43

"If Jesus saves then **he better save himself**
From the gory glory seekers
Who use his name in death."

IAN ANDERSON - JETHRO TULL
ALBUM - AQUALUNG

SONG - Mrs. Robinson

"Now here's to you Mrs. Robinson
Jesus loves you more than you will know
God bless you please Mrs. Robinson
Heaven holds a place for those who pray."
PAUL SIMON/ART GARFUNKEL
ALBUM - Theme to the movie "THE GRADUATE"

SONG - The Blood

"I am paralyzed by the **BLOOD OF CHRIST**
Though it clouds my eyes I can never stop..."
ROBERT SMITH - THE CURE
ALBUM - HEAD ON THE DOOR

SONG - In My Time Of Dying

"Meet me Jesus meet me
Meet me in the middle of the air
If my wings should fail me Lord
Please meet me with another pair -
You can deliver me Lord
I only wanted to have some fun"
ROBERT PLANT - LED ZEPPELIN
ALBUM - PHYSICAL GRAFFITI

SONG - WILD SIDE
"I carry my **crucifix** under my death list
Forward my mail to me in hell -
Our father who ain't in Heaven
Be thy name on the wild side"
VINCE NEIL - MÖTLEY CRÜE
ALBUM - GIRLS GIRLS GIRLS

SONG - Disturbing The Priest

"Good life is a contradiction
Because of the CRUCIFIXION
If you're ready and have the need
I will take YOUR SOUL and plant my seed"

IAN GILLIAN - BLACK SABBATH
ALBUM - BORN AGAIN

SONG - Hell Awaits

"Angels fighting aimlessly
Still dying by the sword
Our Legions killing all in sight
To get the one called Lord...
Jesus knows your soul cannot be saved
Crucify the *so called Lord*
HE SOON SHALL FALL TO ME
Your souls are damned your God has fell
To slave for me eternally

TOM ARAYA - SLAYER
ALBUM - HELL AWAITS

SONG - Imitation of Christ

"Jesus is a *WOMAN* too
He loves like me and all of you --
Imitation of Christ"

RICHARD BUTLER - PSYCHEDELIC FURS
ALBUM - PSYCHEDELIC FURS

SONG - (Don't Need) Religion

"I don't need no blind belief
I don't need no comic relief
I don't need to see those *SCARS*

159

I don't need Jesus Christ superstar
Don't need Sunday television
You bet your life **I don't need religion**"
                    LEMMY KILMISTER - MOTORHEAD
                    ALBUM - IRON FIST

                    SONG - Orgasmatron

"Obsequious and arrogant, clandestine and vain
2000 years of misery, torture in my name
Hypocrisy made paramount, paranoia the law
My name is called *RELIGION,* sadistic, sacred whore"
                    LEMMY K. - MOTORHEAD
                    ALBUM ORGASMATRON

                    SONG - Pray for Death

"Organized religion is deaf, dumb, and blind
They think they see through God's eyes --
It'll be too late when they finally see the light"
                    GROUP - HEATHEN
                    ALBUM - BREAKING THE SILENCE

                    SONG - Religious Vomit

"All religions make me wanna throw up
All religions make me sick
All religions make me wanna throw up
All religions suck"
                    JELLO BIAFRA - DEAD KENNEDYS
                    ALBUM - IN GOD WE TRUST

SONG - The Watchmen

"Kthulhu calls
You'll see, you'll see her
When she starts to form
You'll see, you'll see her
When she starts to call
In the NAME OF *JESUS CHRIST*
Won't you fear my name
I've been around since *MOSES*
Your preacher never came"

CARL McCOY - FIELDS OF THE NEPHILIM
ALBUM - THE NEPHILIM

SONG - Blasphemous Rumours

"I don't want to start any blasphemous rumours
But I think that *GOD* **has a sick sense of humor**
And when I die I expect to find him laughing"

DEPESCHE MODE
ALBUM - SOME GREAT REWARD

Depesche Mode's recent hit song, "Personal Jesus", is a total mockery of God. They sing, "Your own personal Jesus/Someone to hear your prayers/Someone who cares". The video of this song is all done in mockery of televangelists, as well as ridiculing the idea that someone can actually have a *personal* relationship with Jesus Christ.

SONG - Dear God

"I don't believe in heaven and hell
No saints no sinners no devil as well
No pearly gates no THORNY CROWN --

The Father Son and Holy Ghost
Is just somebody's UNHOLY HOAX --
...If there's one thing **I don't believe in**
[music stops, next line sung by a little child]
It's you - DEAR GOD"

ANDY PARTRIDGE - XTC
ALBUM - SKYLARKING

SONG - Praying To A New God

"There's a big world in the street outside
In their uniform of pride
They've all come to see the STAR from THE EAST
Is he man or BEAST
Decide
Feel like I'm CRUCIFIED still I'm not satisfied
The SECOND COMING is coming anyway...
It's ANOTHER SECOND COMING like it or NOT
You better start praying TO **A NEW GOD**"

JACK HUES - WANG CHUNG
ALBUM - THE WARMER SIDE OF COOL

SONG - MERCEDES BENZ

"Oh Lord, won't you buy me
A night on the town
I'm counting on you Lord
Please don't let me down
Prove that you love me
And *buy the next round*"

JANIS JOPLIN
ALBUM - PEARL

SONG - Jacob's Ladder

"I met a fan dancer down in southside Birmingham
She was running from a fat man selling
Salvation in his hand
Now he's trying to save me
Well I'm doing all right the best that I can
Just another **fallen angel**
Trying to get through the night"

HUEY LEWIS AND THE NEWS
ALBUM - FORE

SONG - Best Of Both Worlds

"You don't have to die to go to heaven
Or hang around to be **BORN AGAIN**
Just tune into what this place has to offer
For we may never be here again"

SAMMY HAGAR - VAN HALEN
ALBUM - 5150

SONG - Lost

"Yaweh [Hebrew for God] promised a conquered land
Dominion over life -- man against man
Mother earth came into conflict
With patriarchal powers
And eyes lit up with hierarchy fed desires"
                    ROGER MIRET - AGNOSTIC FRONT
                    ALBUM - AGNOSTIC FRONT

SONG - The Mercy Seat

"I hear stories from the chamber
How Christ was born into a manger
And like some ragged stranger
Died upon the cross
And might I say it seems so fitting in it's way
He was a carpenter by trade
Or at least *THAT'S WHAT I'M TOLD*"
                    NICK CAVE AND THE BAD SEEDS
                    ALBUM - TENDER PREY

Now before we get into the really repugnant examples, and just in case you might think that by the last lyrical example that Nick Cave might have Christian leanings, here is another song from the same album that tells a different story.

"SONG - Up Jumped The Devil

"O my, O my, what a wretched life
I was born on the day that my poor mother died
I was cut from her belly with a Stanley knife
My daddy did a gig with a drunk midwife...
Who's that yonder all in flames
Dragging behind him a sack of chains
Who's that yonder all in flames
Up jumped the Devil and STAKED HIS CLAIM"
                    NICK CAVE AND THE BAD SEEDS
                    ALBUM - TENDER PREY

Coven album cover "Blessed is the Black" depicting Satanic power overcoming the helpless Jesus.

More than likely, Nick Cave is telling us through his song lyrics who *REALLY* has the claim on his life.

The title of the album which contains these two songs is "Tender Prey". It's clear to me, that unfortunately, in the case of Nick Cave and his group, the Dragon has made "tender prey" of a few more human souls.

FROM BAD TO WORSE

The lyrics you are about to read make most of these other songs seem *tame* by comparison. They are filled with **HATE**: Hatred for God, hatred for His Son Jesus Christ, and hatred for Christianity. They are not the worst I've discovered, but they are definitely prime examples of the poison that flows within the Dragon's twisted mind and out of the mouths and pens of his children.

COVEN

Rock & Roll removed its mask of feigned innocence a long time ago. The satanic rock group Coven is a very good example of just what its potential has always been. Their debut album is called "Blessed Is The Black". The picture on the album cover depicts the face of a thorn crowned CHRIST. There is a serpent- like tongue sticking out of his mouth which wraps around the body of a figure representing Jesus. The tip of the tongue turns into the figure of the Devil poised over the body ready to sink a large knife into the chest of the ensnared and impotent looking Savior. That description may seem a bit confusing, but that is exactly what this picture shows. This album cover is obviously meant to portray the supposed superiority of the satanic image.

I feel very sorry for the artist who created this picture, but it doesn't surprise me in the least that he would create this type of "art". You see, I've known his father for many years now and he is only drawing what his father has taught him to draw. Who is his father? Who else? Satan.

Groups usually give special mention to certain people on their album cover credits; people who have either helped or inspired them. Because the members of this band are very young, among those they acknowledge are a certain Mr. & Mrs. Babbitt. Who are these mentionables? They are the parents of the guitarist and the drummer, Dean and Neil.

All I can say is God help the poor, spiritually ignorant parents who would allow their sons to be a part of this demonic refuse.

The band Coven also gives special mention on their album jacket to some other people. Among them: SATAN and *JESUS!!!* Another group of people that merit special mention on this album...their female fans who they call "ALL ROCKER *SLUTS*".

Spoken like true children of Hell.

Let these people tell me this group and their music are only a money making venture; obviously they don't have any idea who is actually promoting and writing the music for Coven. Their songs are satanically saturated, dripping with violence, hate, sexual perversion, and anti-Christian venom. Here is just a sample of what I mean:

SONG - Blessed Is The Black

"Taught from birth you'll burn in hell
For all eternity
If you don't pledge your soul to Christ

And serve Him faithfully
Searching deep within yourself
The evil answer lies
You know your heart is black as hell
And death is in your eyes...
Preachers of the holy gospel
EVANGELISTS OF LIES
Blessed are the men in black
Who see through their disguise

SONG - Burn The Cross

"Tormented Christian sons of God
Lie cold within the grave
Tortured and then sacrificed
For a God they thought to save...
Sons of God repent your sins
And pledge your soul to hell
Pray that Satan will forgive
Once your God has fell
Expect the death of those who pray
To a God so long since passed
YOUR GOD IS *DEAD* AND NOW YOU DIE
Satan rules at last"

Now those examples might seem repulsive enough, but actually, I saved the worst for last. God help their charred souls for writing songs like these!

** WARNING TO THE SENSITIVE **

These lyrics are HIGHLY **OFFENSIVE**. You may want to just skip over them and go on! You have been warned, **read at your own risk.**

SONG - 6669

"Copulation with a corpse
Demons rape her rotting hole
F__ked and left to die -
Virgin b_tch of Christian faith
Serves as Satan's slut
Seduction of the Holy Father
Casting Satan's spell
Tortured and then CRUCIFIED
His soul shall rot in hell"

PAUL HASH - COVEN

The majority of the lyrics for Coven have been written by guitarist Paul Hash. God help his evil soul. I would highly suggest he turn to Jesus...AND HE BETTER DO IT *FAST*!

I think by now you can see how far Rock & Roll has come in just a few short decades.

To prove my point regarding their common origin, I have purposefully used examples from a vast range of musical styles. From rock to pop to heavy metal to punk to funk to rap to new wave music; it is painfully clear that the Dragon's breath emanates from them all.

THE DOWNBOUND TRAIN

Even teenage heart-throb Jon Bon Jovi and his group have climbed aboard the anti-Bible band wagon. On one album you find them singing about "living on a prayer", but on another you find them expressing their open contempt for the Word of God. What do I mean? Let's take a look.

One of their latest hit videos at the time of this writing is of a song from their "New Jersey" album entitled, "Living in Sin". The theme of this song is a rather old one: If a man and a woman "love" each other and want to live together without being married why should anyone else have anything to say about it? It's their lives! They should be allowed to do whatever they want.

Here are a few lines from their song attacking the God-given institution of marriage. Jon sings:

> "I don't need no license
> To sign on no line
> And I DON'T NEED NO PREACHER
> To tell me your mine...
> And your daddy don't approve
> But I don't need your daddy
> Telling us what we should do"

LIVING IN SIN - BON JOVI

Well, Jon Bon Jovi may sing about God, but obviously he has yet to *MEET* Him. If he really *DID* know God he could never sing a song which inspires such rebellion. Rebel against your minister and your father, and live any way you want no matter *what* the Bible says: That is the Bon Jovi answer to life and happiness. That, however, is very bad advice indeed.

God calls sex outside of marriage "FORNICATION". The Bible says "fornicators will **NOT** inherit the kingdom of God" (I Cor. 6:9,10).

There is also another song on the same album that contains a similar well used theme by many of rock's rebels. The song is entitled, "Homebound Train". Does this sound familiar?...

"When I was just a boy
The DEVIL TOOK MY HAND
Took me from my home
He made me a man"

HOMEBOUND TRAIN - BON JOVI

...I thought it would. It seems the Devil, according to Jon, was the one who taught him all about life in his early years.

Obviously the songs of Jon Bon Jovi and his group are rife with spiritual contradiction: One minute Jon is praying to God, the next he's holding hands with the DEVIL. **You can't do *BOTH*!** But I can understand why he would be a bit *confused*. The plain fact is that their god is not the one who WROTE the Bible; he is the god who HATES the Bible. The god of CONFUSION, murder, sin and death...Satan.

There is another interesting line in the song "Homebound Train". It says:

I'm going down down down
Down down
On that homebound train"

It seems to me I've heard *another* **Bon**, besides Bon Jovi, sing a song about going down somewhere. The song this other Bon sang is called "Highway To Hell". It was recorded by some of the Dragon's best friends: The hard rock group AC/DC. Who was the Bon who sang this song?? -- Bon Scott their former lead singer. What was he singing about? Read it and weep:

"Hey, SATAN, paid my dues
Playing in a rockin' band
Hey, mama, look at me
I'm on my way to the PROMISED LAND
I'm on the HIGHWAY TO HELL
Highway to hell
Highway to hell
Highway to hell
Mmmmm don't stop me"

HIGHWAY TO HELL - AC/DC

170

Though I know God sent many messengers across the path of Bon Scott to warn him not to take the "Highway to Hell", it proved to be of no avail. Unfortunately for him, Bon has already climbed aboard the *REAL* downbound train and ridden it to the end of the line. The inferno he now occupies and previously called his "promised land" is one that I would not wish on my worst enemy.

Well, right now you're probably wondering why I would equate two such different people: Bon Scott and Jon Bon Jovi. Once again I'm glad you asked. You see they really aren't that much different.

Bon Scott, the now deceased lead singer for AC/DC, was well known as a drugged-out, hell raising rebel who ended up selling his soul for Rock & Roll. While he was on Earth, he was a permanent resident of "SIN CITY" (the title of one of AC/DC's hit songs).

Now I'm not necessarily saying that Jon Bon Jovi is a drugged-out hell raiser bent on destruction, although, with rebellious songs like "Living in Sin", it is quite obvious "SIN CITY" is also *his* present address. In his case, the story goes much deeper than that.

Here is a little piece of information you might find a bit shocking. In an interview with *Smash Hits* magazine, it seems that Jon let his "boy-next-door" image slip just a little bit when he made a rather candid statement concerning his *total* dedication to Rock & Roll.

Here is a direct quote from one of the most popular Rock & Roll musicians in the world. He said:

"I love my family dearly of course but I'D KILL MY MOTHER FOR ROCK & ROLL. I WOULD SELL MY SOUL. - That's a pretty sick thing to say but I've said some pretty weird stuff to myself you know. Like I'd give a day of my life for every day I can sing good. That's how much I dig it."[24]

JON BON JOVI

Jon said he would trade a day of his life for every day he could "sing good". That is truly a sad perspective on the value of life; but -- *kill* his mother? *Sell* his soul!!? -- That's a whole different story. Bon Scott has *already* sold his soul for Rock & Roll and it seems that Bon Jovi is obviously willing to do the same.

Is there really *that* much difference between the two Bons...not really. So far, they have both served the Dragon well.

When I read things like that last quote from Jon Bon Jovi it makes me feel very sad. Obviously there is something missing in his life that he thinks Rock & Roll will supply.

He is WRONG.

Bon (Scott) has already crashed and burned on the "Highway To Hell" but Jon can still get off that infernal road while there is still time.

JON...**LISTEN**...DON'T SELL YOUR SOUL FOR ROCK & ROLL! IT'S *NOT* WORTH IT!!!

CONCLUSION OF CHAPTER

With all the reprehensible darkness that I have just subjected you to, I think it would only be fair to allow you to exit this chapter on a different note. Read on and you'll understand what I mean.

THE DEMISE OF CAPTAIN LIGHT

Who is Captain Light you might ask? It's a long...long story. For this book, however, I will shorten it quite a bit.

Long before I came to know Jesus Christ, I held a strong fascination for outer space and UFO's. I was also heavily involved in playing Rock & Roll. Somewhere down the line in my life I had planned to meld these two ideas together. I had played in, and formed a number of rock bands all over the country; groups with names such as: The Hard Road, Nebula, Psylense (pron. silence), West Coast South, Parsec, and Billion Bolts Wide, eventually shortened to Bolts. The final incarnation in the evolution of drummer and lead singer Mark Spaulding was to have been the band VISITOR. The leader of the band -- my alter ego, spaceman and outlander, Captain Light.

During the fifteen years of my musical career I had written dozens of songs and even some short stories in preparation for the day that Captain Light would arise.

I had designed a drum set and a stage production that was so unusual that it would have guaranteed me the attention of my audience and my peers. I planned to descend onto the stage from a flying saucer full of flashing colored lights and sing songs about extraterrestrial visitors, light, love, and peace. Though my songs were written to promote altruistic ideals and didn't appear to be evil, in reality they were just as dark and deceptive as many of the ones that you have already read in this book. They just weren't evil in quite the same way.

You see, my songs had also been written under the influence of the Dragon. We had become well acquainted with each other during our many years together. However, it might interest you to know he had not come to me wearing his repulsive and obvious satanic mask of death, darkness, blood, fire and black magic; he wooed me instead by donning his radiant, and well polished New Age "angel of light" disguise. What the Devil had offered *ME* was the same thing he eventually offers every New Ager: The tempting fruit of self-realized godhood, which for any fallible human being is a tempting fruit indeed.

Many people were specifically sent across my path to bring affirmation to my developing godhood. The experiences I had during these encounters could only be classified as supernatural. I was surrounded by people who became my constant companions and exhibited incredible musical and psychic abilities, the likes of which astounded me.

Just as many other musicians write songs about their spiritual experiences, my experiences were also reflected in my music. My song notebook was filled with New Age gems such as these:

1978 Peace Plea

"Love yourself and you will love all
Understand the life and listen to the call
Being one of the truthful lives
It's important just to be
Look around you at your brothers and sisters
And realize what you see
Pretend that you haven't learned to hate
Make believe that you can't kill
Become your **inside sleeping goodness**
Let that control your will"

And:

THE REASON [My first 45 rpm single]

"Let's celebrate the birthday
For the reason that we live
Generators all of us
For the causes that we give
Capturing your feelings
In the reflections of our eyes
And beaming in our sunlight
Through your wicked web of sighs
But I know you're just looking for
The stars up in the sky
Looking for the reason--WHY?

Now that you can feel us
In the corners of your mind
There's no need for stealing
The thing that's there you'll find
We all know the answer
And I think you know it too
Just come back to the beginning
And you'll know just what to do
The time has passed for looking
For the stars up in the sky
We all know the reason why.

Without a doubt, I *knew* I was on the path to *enlightenment*.

Now, I understand that the sentiments put forth in these songs that promote peace and love are not at all evil; but the belief that man can in any way search within and somehow requisition the innate ability to make the necessary changes in character to control the human will and create absolute love, is deception at its very core. You see I believed the same old fallacy that most people who are involved in the various branches of New Age mystical humanism also choose to believe. I believed that we *could* find ultimate goodness within ourselves if we just looked deeply enough. That is honestly what I believed; however, I made one small, but highly significant, error in my personal evaluation of the human spiritual condition. The Bible tells us that as human beings in this world, born into sin, we are born with a fallen nature. The Bible also says there is *"NONE GOOD BUT ONE, THAT IS GOD"* (Mark 10:18)...but I had never read the Bible -- so I didn't know. The Dragon told me the same lie he told Adam and Eve: You are your own god; and just like every other New Age practitioner, I swallowed the bait hook, line, and sinker. With me, however, he took it even one step further. He eventually told me I *WAS* GOD! (Now, don't think this idea is all that unusual. India happens to be overflowing with men and women who think exactly the same thing about themselves--and their followers...well, they believe it too. Not to mention the superstar of Hollywood New Agers, author, actress, occult teacher, metaphysician, and UFO advocate Shirley Maclaine who has also been self-deified. Those who watched her movie special a few years ago entitled, "Out On A Limb", saw her proclaim, as she stood on the beach facing the Pacific Ocean, "I AM GOD".)

The future that the Dragon designed for me was also filled with UFO's, cosmic vibrations, occult New Age power, and to cap it all off, eternal Godhood. I had already tasted of the Dragon's power in my life many times before. There were a few rare occasions where he had bestowed on me the ability to perform feats of "elemental magic". Yes, a few times I can vividly recall I had actually exhibited power over the natural forces of lightning, wind, and rain. This meteorologic power was only a taste of what I could have wielded, had I fully surrendered to the Dragon's plan.

As far as I can conclude by my study of the scriptures, God has never withdrawn the power that he gave to Satan over the elements. He demonstrated this power quite violently and effectively, I might add, against Job when he used it to murder most of Job's family (Job 1:16,19); and remember, as we mentioned earlier (Ch. 1), he can give his powers to whomsoever he chooses. You can call the experiences I had with elemental magic products of a vivid imagination or grandiose delusion if you like; I know what I heard and saw. The Dragon was just giving me a little taste of his special brand of "soul candy" while training me to serve.

Captain Light, just like all the other self-proclaimed messiahs, would not have been able to save the world, anybody in it, or even...himself. He would have only been able to lead his followers on a false path; not one of love, peace, and truth as I had anticipated, but one of darkness that would inevitably lead to destruction. I really thought I had the answers...I was *WRONG*.

Well, that had been the Dragon's plan for my life. I thank God that *HE* had a much better one in store for me instead. After I had invited Christ into my heart, the Lord told me why I had been born into the world in the first place. I had been birthed to preach the GOSPEL. I may have received temporary success, fame, and glory as Captain Light, but it would have been fleeting. The glory that Satan gives always does two things. First, it dissipates. Then, it disappears! The glory that God will eventually be giving me will *NEVER* fade away. IT WILL BE ETERNAL!! Praise God!

The night I walked away from the darkness, God began to fill me with His LIGHT. That night when I gave up the dream of becoming Captain Light, and surrendered my whole life to Jesus Christ, I met the *REAL* CAPTAIN LIGHT: The **Captain** of my salvation who is the **Light** of the world.

As far as my music was concerned, I knew that He would have to be the Captain of that as well. I prayerfully examined all the songs that I had written over that fifteen year period of my life as a musician, and came to the quick realization that *NONE* of them had come from God. Though I still had a deep feeling in my heart for these songs, I knew what I had to do. I took the special notebook, which had been my constant companion for many years, filled with the stories and the songs that I had once cherished and threw it away. It felt like I was discarding a big part of my soul, but I knew they weren't actually mine. Just like *ALL* music that does not find its origin in God...they belonged to the Dragon. They had, in reality, come from him and had nothing whatsoever to do with God.

That, however, is not the end of my musical story. When you are sincere with God, willing to let go of your past, and submit *TOTALLY* to Him, He will ALWAYS give you some of His LIGHT to replace the darkness you are willing to abandon. Though my old songs, the ones that came from the Dragon's heart, are now gone forever, God has given me some new ones that glorify Him to take their place. That is the true purpose of music: TO *GLORIFY* GOD. These new songs don't reflect the heartbeat of the Dragon, instead they reflect the heartbeat of a loving and caring Eternal Father who is reaching out to the lost.

Here is just one of these gifts He has given to me; a song that can actually give life and hope to a dead soul:

SONG - In The Beginning, The WORD

"He was in the beginning
When it all began
When He made the worlds
By the power of His hand
Yes, in the beginning
He made every beast and bird
And He upholds all things even now
By the power of His WORD

The power of His WORD is Spirit
The power of His WORD is Life to us all
The power of His WORD is everlasting love
To redeem us from the fall
And He promised you forever
If you'll just trust in Him
Just reach out your hand to JESUS
And your forever will begin

He said His name was Jesus
He's the MASTER of all things
And if you come to Him He'll shelter you
As with mighty eagle's wings
He loves us each and every one
Became sin for us all
All your burdens will be lifted now
If you only listen to His call

The power of His WORD will change you
The power of His WORD will make your path straight
The power of His WORD will resurrect your love
And CRUCIFY YOUR HATE
So turn your back on all the darkness
For Satan's kingdom it will fail
Just let the loving Savior guide you
Against all evil you'll prevail

You're saved only by believing
It's as simple as can be
Jesus Christ one day left Heaven
Came to earth and died for you and me
He wants you to know He loves you
And He wants to cleanse your sin
He's right here now just to save you
Won't you open up your heart
And let Him in

The power of His WORD will free you
The power of His WORD will break every chain
The power of His WORD will heal your loneliness
And take away your pain
So won't you just believe His promise
It worked for me and can for you
Just reach out your hand to JESUS
For all His promises are true"

CHAPTER 12

WOODSTOCK -- WE ARE THE WORLD

-The Beginning of the End-

"I came upon a child of God
He was walking along the road
And I asked him, where are you going
And this he told me
I'm going on down to Yasgurs' farm
I'm going to join in a rock 'n' roll band
I'm going to camp out on the land
And try an' get my soul free"

WOODSTOCK - JONI MITCHELL

Three days of fun and music...and I God bless you for it."

MAX YASGUR
OWNER OF WOODSTOCK FESTIVAL SITE

Contrary to folk singer Joni Mitchell's tribute song, a verse of which you have just read, and Mr. Yasgur's invoked blessing, which he so graciously pronounced on those attending the Woodstock Music and Arts Festival, the people at Woodstock not only failed in freeing their souls, they also failed to receive God's blessing for their behavior. God was not *about* to bless those involved. He knew what was *REALLY* going on there, and He was not at all **pleased**.

Satan knew about Woodstock as well - he was *promoting* it. He knew that before his final battle with the LORD, that his beloved Babylon, land of sin and idolatry, must rise once more. We have witnessed this occurrence in our present generation. It was born of flesh in 1969 naked, high, and tranced-out. During one short three day period of time, the Dragon captured a half-a- million souls with one giant sweep of his monstrous tail. Three days of peace, love, and music, would more appropriately be remembered as three days of lust, sorcery, and pantheistic ritual.

As I watched T.V. reports, read magazine articles, and viewed a rescreening of the Woodstock movie on MTV, I couldn't help but marvel at the accolades showered upon this unprecedented event. Reporter after reporter, and interviewer after interviewer, universally attested to the fact that Woodstock had been a massive shift in the consciousness of our nation. With this evaluation, I couldn't agree more. It was just exactly the shift of consciousness (mass possession, if you will) necessary to truly usher in the Golden Age...of the anti-Christ.

At the time of this writing, America has just recently celebrated the 20th anniversary of Woodstock. Since I don't really have the space to go into great detail about all the things that actually took place at this music and arts festival, I will just zero in on some of the highlights.

As you view the Woodstock movie, it is not difficult to tell that the young people attending the festival took extreme pleasure in breaking all the basic social rules.

Taking drugs was only one aspect of their rebellion, but it is a safe estimation that *most* of the people at Woodstock were stoned on something. LSD, THC, MDA, STP, pot, hashish, heroin, opium, mescaline, psilocybin, peyote, and PCP were just some of the illegal drugs which were readily available to everyone. A short drink from a pass-around wine or soft-drink bottle to quench a parched throat guaranteed one a psychedelic experience whether they wanted one or not. Everything, including the drinking water, was tainted with any number of mind-altering drugs. Even the police officers assigned to keep things under control around the stage area, after drinking a cup of coffee or water, a short time later found themselves trying to cope with uninvited feelings of drug induced euphoria and hallucinations. The whole place was literally on one big *TRIP*.

In this ecstatic state of pharmaceutical exhilaration, sexual mores were also quickly abandoned. But apart from the fact that there was rampant public nudity as well as the proclivity for open sexual promiscuity, some people attending Woodstock were stepping *WAY* over the line. Now, it's one thing to break the rules, but it's yet another to *SHATTER TABOOS*. One man attending the festival was blatantly doing both. *Rolling Stone* magazine carried his story in their special Woodstock edition. When I first read about this man and the degrading doctrine he was preaching to the young and impressionable music worshipers attending the festival, I was, to put it mildly, SHOCKED..but yet in a way, not surprised. What *am* I talking about? Glad you asked. Here is the true story of the witch and his "wife". Now **YOU** prepare for a shock!

"LOVING" THE LAMB

In the Woodstock movie, as well as in some photos recently shown in the *Life* magazine, August 1989, Woodstock memory issue, is a picture of an interesting looking man holding a staff, of sorts, topped by a HUMAN SKULL. From the staff hangs a sign that reads, "DON'T EAT ANIMALS, LOVE THEM/THE KILLING OF ANIMALS CREATES THE KILLING OF MEN". The man in the picture is Louie Moonfire. He is a WARLOCK (male witch). When Moonfire expressed his sentiments about "loving" animals, many people active in the fight for animal rights would tend to applaud what appeared on the surface to be such a caring and admirably humane proclamation. But most people would never have possibly imagined that when he said "love them" what he actually was refering to was MAKING LOVE *TO* THEM! Allow me to clarify this a little further.

In the book entitled 20 Years of Rolling Stone is a reprint of an article that had previously been written about the Woodstock festival back in 1969. Here is a brief excerpt from this article:

> "Moonfire, a warlock, preached to a small crowd of people that had gathered under the stage for shelter. A tall man with red-brown hair and shining eyes, barefoot and naked under his robes, he had traveled to the festival with his *LOVER* A SHEEP...He carefully explained how sheep were blessed with the greatest capacity of love of all animals, how a sheep could *CONCEIVE BY A MAN*, though tragically, because of some forgotten curse, the offspring was doomed to die at BIRTH."[1]

Woodstock warlock, Moonfire, promoting his "love" animals doctrine.

Do you fully understand what you just read?? This male witch was FORNI-CATING REGULARLY WITH HIS PET LAMB!!! He was also upset that the cursed thing *birthed* by the sheep would not *LIVE!*

This abominable act of having sexual intercourse with animals is called bestiality. Bestiality was an incredibly perverted sin practiced not only in Babylon, but also in Egypt, India, and the Canaanite nations, including the iniquitous cities of Sodom and Gomorrah. It was expressly forbidden by God, and under His law, punishable by death. The Bible states:

"Whosoever lieth with a beast shall surely be put to death."
Exodus 22:19

Despite the fact that many researchers believe that sexually transmitted diseases entered into the human sphere as a result of bestiality, as well as the fact that this repulsive satanic practice is clearly cursed by God, this Woodstock warlock was proclaiming the *BENEFITS* of bestiality to the crowd.

Wherever you find drugs and tantric sexual behavior, will the yogis be far away? Not on a bet. The Woodstock movie also included scenes of Kundalini yoga instructor, Tom Law, teaching his ancient techniques to a crowd of young would-be gurus. Law remembers:

"A number of times, Wavy would ask me to lead everyone in yoga from the stage. I would come over and fill in for fifteen or twenty minutes. I would just talk about 'Here's another way to get high. No drugs. Try this.' I was just having everybody sit up straight. You don't have to be in the lotus pose, but basically sit up with your legs crossed in front of you and take these deep breaths and then exhale them completely and squeeze all the air out. And I was having them raising their hands up..."[2]

Tom Law was not the only yogi at Woodstock. Indian Yoga master Swami Satchadinanda and his whole entourage also took the stage to teach the crowd of 100,000+ the Hindu philosophy of life. The young festival attendees were extremely receptive to his message. Satchadinanda noticed there was very little difference between his religious ideals and the ones being exhibited at Woodstock. He was pleasantly surprised to witness a Hindu indoctrination taking place in America on a much larger scale than he had anticipated. Yes, Hinduism was also being fervently preached at Woodstock.

One of the performers, a singer named Melanie, recalled, in one interview, having an out-of-body experience just before she went on stage to sing. She remembers actually floating around at the side of the stage while watching her body sing and play guitar. (Remember, astral projection, as we have mentioned earlier, is another Hindu technique.) With all the drugs being consumed and all the Hindu meditation taking place, I'm sure Melanie was not the only one experiencing such things. Without a doubt, there were plenty of similar spiritual experiences that have never been reported.

I might also briefly mention the now famous "rain chant" incident, where a vast number of people began methodically tapping out a rhythm with bottles, sticks, cans, and anything else that would make a noise; dancing, and chanting in unison. This occurrence was both shown in the movie and recorded on the soundtrack album. You may find it interesting to know that beating out a rhythm on bottles and cans while chanting, like the people were doing in the Woodstock episode, is exactly the same way that the people of Bahia, Brazil prepare themselves for their Candomblé **spirit possession rituals**. Another coincidental correlation??? Not likely. The demonic spirits running Woodstock were obviously having a field day.

TRUE PEACE

There was also a lot of talk about peace at Woodstock. Now I can't fault anyone for desiring peace in this routinely war- filled and troubled world, but I *can* ask a legitimate question: Will peace actually come in our day?? The answer: YES...and no.

A charismatic man appearing to represent peace will soon appear upon the world scene, but his hidden agenda will actually be one of war. Initially he will fool the people into believing that he is an emissary of peace, but tragically most of those who believe his lies will eventually perish.

Peace will never come by rebelling against God and His laws. This rebellion will only, in turn, construct a spiritual fortress of darkness, imprisoning those involved. This dark prison can be successfully penetrated by only *one* LIGHT. He alone can lead the way out for those desiring to make their escape into the TRUTH. That LIGHT is **Jesus Christ**: The Living and True God; the *ONLY* God that the Woodstock nation and their guru fathers absolutely *REFUSE* to worship.

Maybe that is why the Dragon picked the same man who played a major part in the production of this clearly anti-Christian movie, "Woodstock", to also create another anti-Christian film, which saw its infamous release in the late summer of 1988. It is the most blasphemous film about Jesus Christ to ever spew its poison images upon the silver screen. Martin Scorsese, the man who presented us with the abomination entitled, "The Last Temptation of Christ", was also the same man who helped create the movie "Woodstock"! ...Another interesting and unusual connection, wouldn't you say?

The occult, drug-induced altered states of consciousness, ritual music and ritual dress (or more noticeably ritual *UNDRESS:* nudity playing an important role in yoga and witchcraft), meditation, sorcery, yogic trance, and mass possession was the gospel that the Dragon wanted preached throughout this "Christian" country. With a half-a-million young, and in many cases quite naive, Woodstock evangelists and their musical gurus who were specifically trained to do the proselytizing, that is exactly what he got.

Lastly, it is also interesting to note that the festival was actually not even held in Woodstock. It was held in a place called Bethel, New York. Bethel, in the Hebrew language of the Old Testament, means "the house of God". This obviously adds a touch of irony to the story, for during those three days, the farmlands and fields of Bethel truly housed *many* gods...all of them FALSE. I can hear the Dragon laughing now.

All this darkness aside, however, in the same *Life* magazine 20th anniversary Woodstock article mentioned earlier in this chapter, there shines a bright ray of hope. It shines from a man who was at the festival and saw it all. His name is Paul Foster, a former member of the "hog farm" commune run by a person named Wavy Gravy who also helped organize and run Woodstock (Wavy Gravy [real name Hugh Romney] is the man pictured in the Woodstock movie saying 'What we have in mind is breakfast in bed for 400,000'). You wouldn't have seen Paul Foster interviewed on all those Woodstock memorial shows because this present global-minded generation, spawned in a sea of drugs and mud, doesn't want to hear what he *now* has to say. So I will tell you what he says, because as far as I can ascertain, he is the only one of all those interviewed who has actually escaped the spiritual deception of Woodstock. Here are his own words:

> "I was always on a quest. I tried everything. I was a Jew, I studied the Sikh religion in India, and I entered a Hindu monastery...I tried lots of drugs. None of it worked...The kids of that time were unhappy with what their parents had given them - they wanted something more. I *found* that something more in my **faith in CHRIST.**"[3]

> PAUL FOSTER

Paul Foster found the answer he sought because he was willing to open his heart to the TRUTH. To all the Woodstock alumni who have kept up the search for the truth, and to anyone else who may still be looking, you need look no further than Jesus Christ. He said:

> *"I AM THE WAY, THE TRUTH, AND THE LIFE: NOBODY COMES TO THE FATHER, BUT BY ME"*

> John 14:6

Yes, JESUS CHRIST is the one who will soon strike the final death blow that will pierce the dark heart of the Dragon...FOREVER! The Bible foretells the downfall of the Evil One. God's Word says concerning this final confrontation:

> *"In that day the LORD with his sore and great strong sword shall punish leviathan the piercing serpent, even leviathan that crooked serpent; and he shall* **SLAY THE DRAGON** *that is in the sea."*
>
> Isaiah 27:1

That will be a joyous moment indeed and one that I anxiously anticipate, but for the time being, the Serpent is still promoting his lies.

Since Woodstock, there have been many mini-Woodstock events which we will discuss in the next chapter, but without question, Woodstock was one massive celebration orchestrated by the Dragon himself. He took extreme delight in watching his Rock & Roll children of the new Babylon beginning to mature.

Where has the road from Woodstock led us? That is what we are about to answer.

CHAPTER 13

NEW AGE MUSIC - CROSSING THE RAINBOW BRIDGE

"We are stardust we are golden
We are caught in the Devil's bargain
And we've got to get ourselves
Back to the garden"

WOODSTOCK - JONI MITCHELL

The lyrics you have just read are taken from the same song, "Woodstock", written by folk singer Joni Mitchell that opened the previous chapter. This song, later recorded by Woodstock veterans David Crosby, Stephen Stills, and Graham Nash, along with compatriot Neil Young was composed as a tribute to commemorate the New Age pagan Rock & Roll celebration about which you just read.

Though lyrics in the song such as, "We are stardust, we are golden", are far from being accurate in their description of the human condition; other lyrics in the song are nevertheless true. It is a fact, as the song declares, we *ARE* "caught in the Devil's bargain" (though "rip-off" would be a more accurate description). The sinful human race has not only collectively fallen out of fellowship with a HOLY God, but we are also totally devoid of the innate ability to facilitate our own spiritual redemption. But do not be dismayed. Just because it is impossible for *us* to recover ourselves from the Devil's snare does not mean it cannot be done. I know someone who can do it for us. He can lead us into a beautiful

GARDEN in a kingdom more glorious than anyone can imagine. The *GOOD NEWS* is yet to come...so stay tuned.

This chapter is specifically included in this book because of a relatively new musical phenomenon which is at this present time sweeping the country: New Age music. Though this subject could easily require a volume of its own to do it justice, I felt that this writing would not be complete without a brief mention of this latest musical genre.

In the last few chapters we have mentioned the New Age many times. To understand the concept of New Age music it is important to have a basic understanding of what is meant by the NEW AGE.

THE NEW AGE/HINDU CONNECTION

In the New Age Movement as well as in the religion of Hinduism, two definite things are consistently experienced by its hierophants. One, the participant will often through yoga, meditation, drugs, etc., enter an altered state of consciousness during which he or she encounters discarnate entities or spirit- beings; and two, these experiences not only radically alter the subject's world view, but this alteration produces a proclivity toward anti-Christian spirituality and anti-biblical behavior. Hinduism and New Age dogma share this transitional experience. In essence, these two belief systems are one and the same.

There is certain music that enhances and in may cases instigates the same type of spiritual transformation as that experienced by the adepts of Hinduism. It is called New Age music. Strictly, by definition, New Age music is any music designed to produce in the mind and spirit of the listener either the altered state, the altered world view, or both.

The term "New Age music" then can either be used in a very broad and sweeping sense, or it can focus specifically on a particular mode of musical composition. For most people familiar with the term, it represents a more jazz oriented or ethereal sound which transports the soul of the listener into an alternative spiritual dimension, not unlike that which is experienced by the yogi or shaman in trance state. That is probably the most accepted view in the identification of New Age music. However, that ethereal, trance inducing style is not the only mode of music which can be identified as New Age.

Rock & Roll, in one way or another, has also been involved in indoctrinating the general public with New Age thinking. On the surface, the Rock & Roll/New Age connection may not be quite as overt as the Rock & Roll/occult connection, but it is essentially the same and equally as dangerous. Let's take a closer look at another aspect of the Dragon's master plan.

RAINBOW BRIDGE

Most people familiar with New Age terminology are aware of the great significance of the words "Rainbow Bridge". To explain it briefly, the Rainbow Bridge is a spiritual concept, a spiritual bridge, if you will, which New Age advocates claim connects the "God-self" in every person to the "universal mind", also known as the *OVER-SOUL*. One New Age teacher explains it this way, "It is the bridge between the personality and the 'higher-self'".

The teaching of the Rainbow Bridge, also called by its esoteric name, *ANTAHKARANA*, was put forth in the writings of New Age leader and teacher, Alice Bailey.

Much of the information in Bailey's books was supplied to her supernaturally by spirit entities called "the Masters of Wisdom". They represented themselves to her as ascended or advanced souls who had previously experienced a vast number of lifetimes or incarnations, who were now attempting to communicate their accumulated knowledge and ancient wisdom to those on earth spiritually advanced enough to receive and comprehend it. Though these spirit-beings claimed to be advanced reincarnated souls, they were not at all who they claimed to be. Their true identity can easily be ascertained by a simple examination of their anti- biblical doctrines. They were, in fact, the same fallen angels who have inhabited the earth since the spiritual suicide of man; demonic messengers who were, as in time past, once again using willing human beings as vessels or mediums to spread their anti- Christian and destructive "revelations".

In order to print and distribute her occult teaching material, Bailey founded her own publishing concern aptly named the LUCIFER PUBLISHING COMPANY. Though Lucifer Publishing is still in operation today, it is now called by the new and much less conspicuous name LUCIS TRUST. Located in, of all places, the United Nations Plaza in New York City, it continues to this day to be a prime source for New Age literature.

The Rainbow Bridge concept was but one of the multiplicities of teachings of Alice Bailey finding its theological roots buried deep in the quagmire of Hinduism; one religion definitely being used to turn the human race away from the God of the Bible and toward the eternally deceptive search for the "God-within".

Now the question at hand is this: How does all this information about ascended masters, New Age leaders, and Hindu theology, such as the Rainbow Bridge concept, possibly tie in with Rock & Roll? You are about to find out.

In 1972, a movie was released which was a documentary about the occupants of an occult commune located on the island of Maui, Hawaii, and a special concert which they sponsored. The title of the movie was "Rainbow Bridge". It starred "Voodoo Child" guitarist Jimi Hendrix who came to the island by invitation to help with an experiment that was being conducted by the commune; an occult experiment dealing with color, sound, and "cosmic vibrations". Interestingly enough, the name of the commune, undoubtedly inspired by the teachings of Alice Bailey, was the **Rainbow Bridge** Occult Research Meditation Center.

This Hendrix film was accompanied by a sound track primarily composed of Jimi's songs. It included special New Age compositions he had written especially for this particular performance such as, "Earth Blues", and a song called, "Hey Baby (Land of the New Rising Sun)".

The movie was also filled with occultism previously taught and practiced by Alice Bailey and her followers. The purpose of Bailey's teaching was to initiate the participants on a path of new spirituality -- lead them into a New Age...the Age of Aquarius. The purpose for the "Rainbow Bridge" film was exactly the same. It was saturated with Eastern occult teachings and techniques. Meditation, astral projection, astrology, the worship of Indian yogis and gurus (Paramahansa Yogananda, Lahiri Mahasaya, Meher Baba, and Swami Satchadinanda), mind-altering drugs such as LSD and hashish, chanting the Hindu mantra OM, the doctrine of reincarnation; all these occult ideas were strongly promoted by the movie.

The film, "Rainbow Bridge", was not just another Rock & Roll movie; it was covert propaganda endorsed by a well known and highly respected Rock & Roll star, Jimi Hendrix; specifically designed for the purpose of indoctrinating masses of American youth into a belief in Hindu/New Age theology.

THE GREAT INVOCATION

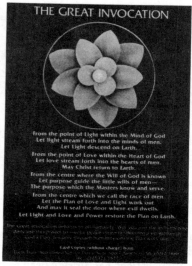

Lucis Trust "Great Invocation" ad from page 203, October, 1982 issue of Reader's Digest.

Though the "Rainbow Bridge" movie did promote all these practices we just mentioned, there is an excerpt in the film that is perhaps even more important for us to understand -- It is the recitation of a special "prayer" called "The Great Invocation". I later learned more about this prayer after seeing it printed in the October 1982 issue of *Reader's Digest*. Since I have begun my research into the New Age movement, I have not only seen the prayer in print, but I have also viewed New Age videos where the narrator recites this invocation in a soothing and almost hypnotic tone of voice. All the while, the viewer is subjected to a number of shifting and flashing geometrical configurations: patterns of light and color dancing across the screen. This video is clearly meant to put the viewer into a trance.

More recently, I have seen "The Great Invocation" in the Winter 1990 issue of a New Age publication called *Meditation* magazine accompanied by a fund

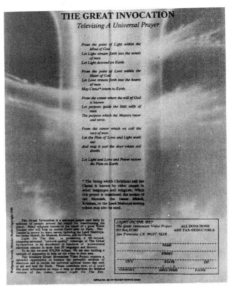

This ad from Meditation Magazine one of the latest ads to promote worldwide recitation of the "Great Invocation": the call to the Antichrist to come forth.

raising advertisement. The ad is being used to raise money for the production of one minute television spots to be aired internationally in many different languages ("The Great Invocation" has already been translated and distributed in 52 different languages). The main thrust of these TV ads will be to solicit global participation in the daily recitation of this prayer.

Before I explain my concern regarding this invocation, I think it would only be fair to allow you to read it.

THE GREAT INVOCATION

"From the point of Light within the mind of God
Let Light stream forth into the minds of men.
Let Light descend on Earth
From the point of Love within the heart of God
Let love stream forth into the hearts of men.
May **Christ** return to Earth.
From the centre where the will of God is known

Let purpose guide the little wills of men -
The purpose which the *Masters* know and serve.
From the centre which we call the race of men
Let the PLAN of Love and Light work out
And may it seal the door where evil dwells.
Let Light and Love and Power restore the *PLAN* on Earth."[1]

Now, on the surface, I realize that this prayer sounds neither ominous nor threatening. As a matter of fact it sounds rather positive; however, the ad in *Meditation* magazine clearly explains the purpose for its use. Here is what it says:

> "**The Great Invocation** is a universal prayer used daily by millions of people around the world for *transforming* the planet. Many religions believe in the return of a great *WORLD TEACHER* who will help us restore God's plan on Earth."[2]

Now, as you can see, this prayer is a call to the "World Teacher" to return to earth. But, *which* World Teacher? That is the question.

Now remember, I just mentioned the fact that 60 second spots were being produced for television airing around the world? Well, the ad says something else you might find rather interesting. It continues:

> "This visionary **Great Invocation** Video Project presents a splendid opportunity to harness the powerful medium of television and to invoke the **universal spiritual forces** that seek to aid and heal the Earth."[3]

Now here is where the problem with the "Invocation" arises. First, the "spiritual forces" being invoked by this prayer are not benevolent by any stretch of the imagination. Secondly, the *CHRIST* that is being invited to take control of the Earth, you may be surprised to find out, is *NOT* necessarily the one with whom we have become the most familiar. This Christ's name does *NOT* happen to be Jesus. As a matter of fact, this Christ has many names. The magazine ad includes a footnote concerning the line in the prayer which reads, "May Christ return to Earth". The footnote regarding the word "*CHRIST*" says:

> "The Being which Christians call the **Christ** is known by other names in other languages and religions. When this prayer is translated, the names of the **Messiah**, the **Imam Mahdi**, **Krishna**, or the **Lord Maitreya** among others may also be used."[4]

In other words, when you recite "The Great Invocation", if you do not believe in Jesus, or biblical Christianity, you can replace the word "Christ" with any religious messianic figure you choose to substitute in its place. This is the pinnacle of deception. The truth is that there is only one name that will save a lost soul . . . *JESUS*. The apostle Peter tells us this fact in the Bible in Acts 4:12. Inspired by the Holy Spirit he says:

> "...*There is NO OTHER NAME under heaven given among men whereby we must be SAVED*."

What then is the "Great Invocation", or should I correctly say *INCANTA-TION?* It is very simply an invitation to a new Christ (i.e. the anti-Christ) to assume the leadership position over all humanity. It is a clarion call for the Dragon to ascend the throne and his government to assume full power. Now, with this information in mind, this little prayer doesn't look quite so benevolent...DOES IT?

As thousands upon thousands of young people, including myself, flocked to movie theaters nationwide to watch their guitar hero Jimi Hendrix flashing across the silver screen, wailing out his Aquarian voodoo riffs on his upside-down white Stratocaster, we were being more than just entertained. We were also being subtly programmed to accept occultism and implement this New Age incantation; and remember, this was back in **1972**, long before Shirley MacLaine made New Age occultism popular.

As you can now clearly see, the "Great Invocation" indoctrination obviously began long before *Reader's Digest* printed the prayer in 1982 (In fact it actually originated in 1945, strangely enough coinciding with the formation of the United Nations). Jimi Hendrix and his "Rainbow Bridge" occult/Rock & Roll movie were destined to play a key role in bringing the New Age "PLAN" mentioned in the "Invocation" to fruition. (For more information on the New Age implementation of the "Plan" promoted by Alice Bailey and her "Masters", read <u>Hidden Dangers of the Rainbow</u> by Constance Cumbey.)

Not only did Jimi Hendrix dialogue in the "Rainbow Bridge" movie about his experiences in astral projection and his belief in reincarnation, but as we mentioned earlier he also wrote a special song for "Rainbow Bridge" as well; a short rap/sing song called, "Hey Baby (Land of the New Rising Sun)". In itself the song title means very little until you discover the name of Jimi's "new rising sun".

In a well known piece of New Age space fantasy called, <u>2010</u>, written by Arthur C. Clarke, also made into a movie of the same name, the name of this "new rising sun" is revealed. It is a name we have discussed already in this book on more than one occasion. Prepare yourself for another surprise. The name of this new sun is...*LUCIFER!*

Hendrix also told Chuck Wein, the initiator and producer of the "Rainbow Bridge" film that anyone "who wanted to could be Jesus". Jimi, unfortunately, believed a lie.

But the saddest thing about the movie "Rainbow Bridge" is the way it begins. One of the stars of the movie, Pat Hartley, is shown being surrounded by a group of people literally ranting and raving about Jesus, the Bible, Hell, and destruction. In the movie Hartley plays the part of someone who is totally turned off by these Bible shaking fanatics and proceeds to explain to them that they are all "hung up on fear". Once again, in typical media fashion, born-again Christians are depicted as insensitive, narrow-minded, Bible-thumping fear mongers. Hopefully, Hartley has since received a more rational presentation of the Gospel, but whether she has or not, it is apparent the movie audience received exactly the impression of Christians and their "archaic" religion that the Dragon wanted them to have: Christianity is **passé** as a viable belief system. Hendrix and his New Age/occult movie "Rainbow Bridge" fulfilled their intended purpose well.

YES--AND THE NEW AGE

Jimi Hendrix was not the only rock musician to embrace the concept of the dawning of a New Age. Jon Anderson and his group, Yes, have also done their share of promoting New Age ideology. Their album, "Tales From Topographic Oceans", is a prime example of what I mean. It was inspired by reading the

The Hindu teachings in the autobiography of a yogi by Guru Paramahansa Yogananda not only affected the group "Yes" but also highly influenced the lives of many other musicians: Elvis, Carlos Santana, and Gary Wright of the group "Spooky Tooth" were just a few who adopted his teachings as their own.

New Age/Hindu book based on the life of Indian Yogi Paramahansa Yogananda. The book is called <u>Autobiography of a Yogi</u>. Yogananda was the guru principally responsible for introducing Hinduism to America as early as 1920. He was also the founder of the Self-Realization Fellowship, a Hindu religious organization. (Self-realization is a key to New Age thinking.) According to Anderson, the Yes album, "Tales", is inspired by some basic Eastern Hindu ideologies taught in Yogananda's book. Evidence concerning the source of this influence is recorded on the inside cover of the album. Jon Anderson writes:

> "We were in Tokyo on tour, and I had a few minutes to myself in a hotel room before the evenings concert. Leafing thru Paramahansa Yogananda's Autobiography of A Yogi I got caught up in the lengthy footnote on page 83. It described the four part Shastric scriptures which cover all aspects of religion and social life as well as fields like medicine and music, art and architecture. For some time, I had been searching for a theme for a large scale composition. So positive in character were the Shastras that I could

Hindu artwork depicting symbols - lotus flower, hexagram (mentioned in Chapter 9), triangle, and coiled Kundalini serpent also represented as a spiral.

visualize there and then, four interlocking pieces of music being structured around them. That was in February. Eight months later, the concept was released and this recording."

As you can read for yourself, Hinduism is once again playing its part in the music and philosophy of one more very popular Rock & Roll group.

A more recent album by Yes entitled, "Big Generator", contains a song called "Holy Lamb". Now it would be wonderful if the Holy Lamb they were singing about was the Holy Lamb of God, Jesus Christ, but that is not the case. In fact, they actually subtitled this same song, "Song for HARMONIC CONVERGENCE". What does this mean? I will explain.

The Harmonic Convergence was a worldwide New Age meditation celebration held on August 16 & 17, 1987 calling together 144,000 (for the true significance of the number 144,000, see Revelation Chapter 7) shamans, witches, firewalkers, gurus, medicine men, and different people from all over the world; other New Agers to chant, meditate, dance, and utter incantations. Once again, as with the aforementioned "Great Invocation", this celebration was held for the purpose of calling down the "Masters" or "spirit guides" to rule the earth. (I think it is a little more than significant that during this same period of time that the help of these spirits was being procured, the second worst airline disaster in United States history occurred. The very night of the "Harmonic Convergence", Northwest Airlines flight 255 crashed on takeoff at Detroit's Metro Airport, killing all the passengers and crew. Only one infant girl was pulled from the wreckage alive. If that's the kind of "help" we receive by invoking these spirits it might not be such a good idea! Help like that <u>WE DON'T NEED</u>!)

Another song on the "Big Generator" album entitled, "Almost Like Love", has Jon Anderson singing:

> "Who was it organizing the right
> To follow my leader
> Seems we look and stand around waiting
> For a sign from God
> Speaking for myself
> The Christian need
> The Muslim need
> The Buddhist need
> To testify the need for brotherly love -
> Please organize our spiritual evolution
> So that you'll feel it
> And we'll feel it --
> Saint or sinner
> MAKES NO DIFFERENCE IN WHO YOU BELIEVE
> In a world of superstition
> Caught in a total nuclear greed"

Though I truly do understand their sentiment, they have made two very big mistakes in this song: one, brotherly love is not the total answer, and two, it does matter a *great deal in whom you BELIEVE*.

On still another album by the group Yes entitled, "Close To The Edge", they also advocate the benefits of Witchcraft. The first song on the album contains the lyrics:

> "A seasoned **witch** could call you
> From the depths of your disgrace

And rearrange your lives
To the solid mental grace"
SONG - THE SOLID TIME OF CHANGE

Even former keyboardist for the group, Rick Wakeman, for a while maintained his New Age ties. Two solo efforts were recorded in 1988, one entitled, "The Family Album", and the other entitled, "Zodiaque", featuring on its cover the twelve astrological symbols of the zodiac. Across the covers of both of these recordings is written, "The Rick Wakeman NEW AGE Collection". The "Zodiaque" tape even includes an insert containing pertinent information about the Babylonian origin of astrology, the name of each astrological sign and the personality traits attributed to persons born in that specific time frame.

Interestingly enough, the "Relativity" label, for which Wakeman recorded these solo projects, uses the *SPIRAL* as its logo. In Hinduism, the lifeblood of the New Age movement, the spiral is a symbol of utmost significance. It represents the **KUNDALINI**, or serpent power which the yogis and gurus say is coiled at the base of the spine. Kundalini Yoga and meditation is practiced to release this serpent power into the brain. This, they inform us, unleashes latent **PSYCHIC** abilities.

With this in mind, it seems that not only was Rick Wakeman's music New Age, but apparently so were the people responsible for its production.

I have recently learned, however, as a result of a brief parousal of CCM magazine, that Rick Wakeman's latest album consists not only of his keyboard music, but his wife can be heard on the tracks reciting verses from the Bible. I have been in contact with personal friends of Mr. Wakeman who have informed me that he and his wife have accepted the Lord Jesus Christ as their Savior. Attempt has been made for verification of this statement from Rick Wakeman himself. As of this date no contact has come about, and Wakeman is once again performing with Yes.

Though I will continue to fervently pray for the salvation of these men, without a doubt you can see that the members of Yes are sympathetic to the ideals and teachings of the New Age movement.

Though I doubt they fully understand the role they play in "The Plan", with all their songs about UFO's, tantra, love, Harmonic Convergence, Witchcraft, Syncretism, and global brotherhood; they are in every sense of the term New Age propagandists. God, open their eyes to the truth.

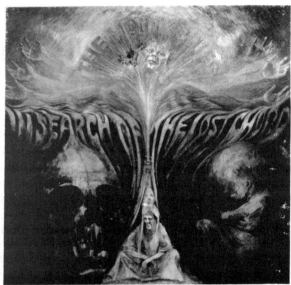

Front cover of Moody Blues album "In Search of the Lost Chord," depicting the reincarnation cycle and meditation as the escape into Nirvana.

NEW AGE FOREFATHERS - THE MOODY BLUES

One of the initial trend setting groups at the very core of the New Age/Rock & Roll connection, which began its musical career way back in the late 1960's, is the Moody Blues.

Though their popularity has waned over the years, this group has done more to promote Hinduism and New Age theology than almost any other Rock & Roll band to date.

Their first big hit entitled, "Go Now", a simple "lost love" ballad released in 1965, was devoid of anything occultic. However, the next big hit entitled, "Knights in White Satin", from their second major release, "Days of Future Passed", accompanied by the London Festival Orchestra, exhibited a subtle change in not only the music, but also in the lyrical style. From the back of the album cover we read these lines of poetic verse included on the album:

"Cold hearted orb that rules the night,
Removes the colours from our sight.
Red is grey and yellow white,
But we decide which one is right.
And which is an ILLUSION???"

Their seemingly abrupt change in style and imagery I believe was due not only to a personnel change (John Lodge and Justin Hayward replacing vocalist Denny Laine and bassist Clint Warwick), but even more so to one *major* contributing factor which altered the way the new Moody Blues perceived reality. Around this time in their recording career they began to attend certain parties where a large number of people, musician friends in particular, got together to collectively experience the benefits of "tripping" on LSD.

Just as in the case of Beatle George Harrison, without a doubt experimentation with this perception altering drug played an important part in enticing the Moody Blues into a courtship with Hinduism. Beginning with their second album, "Days of Future Passed", to the present time, this fact remains apparent.

The third album they recorded was entitled, "In Search of the Lost Chord". This album not only contains songs promoting the teachings of Hinduism, but even the album *cover* makes this purposeful indoctrination quite clear. The front of the album cover visually portrays the concept of reincarnation, with a skull representing death on the left side, and a pre-natal child representing new birth on the right. In the center is the figure of a spiritual master who appears to be in deep contemplation or meditation. His meditation obviously produces the desired results, for in this picture he is suddenly swept upward past the life and death cycles to break through into a transcendant realm that could only be described as the highest level of consciousness. But the Hindu thought being promoted by this album cover doesn't end there. It becomes much clearer on the inside of the album jacket. As you open the cover, you are greeted by a geometrical configuration called a YANTRA, which was briefly mentioned in chapter 10. The purpose for the yantra is explained in some detail so the purchaser of the record will know exactly the message the members of the Moody Blues are trying to promote. They write:

"The Yantra is something which can hold the mind to a form much
as in the less organized way one can see pictures in the glowing
embers of a fire or cloud."

Above: "Lost Chord" inside album cover showing Hindu Yantra and explaining the Yantra and Mantra concepts. As well as the word Mantra OM.
Below: Shakti/Shiva Yantra taken from book The Tantric Way.

That is their explanation of the yantra, but if you remember correctly, when we discussed it in an earlier chapter of this book (chapter 10) we had previously determined its use has quite a different purpose. Yantras are visual aids for worshiping and communing with specific Hindu deities. This is the true purpose of the yantra.

THERE'S NO PLACE LIKE OM

Not only does this album cover, "Chord", mention the yantra, but is also mentions something called a MANTRA. A mantra is a word or group of words or sounds chanted by gurus and yogis over and over again, for hours or even days at a time. This repetitious chanting is not only meant to produce a change of consciousness in the one uttering the mantra, but once again it is designed to attract specific spirit entities. It is the sound equivalent of the deity it represents. The mantra is quite simply a prayer to demon gods. A good example would be, "Hare Krishna Hare Krishna/Krishna Krishna Hare Hare/Hare Rama Hare Rama/Rama Rama Hare Hare". Participation in the chanting of Hindu mantras is precisely what the Moody Blues were promoting on their album. On the inside cover it also states:

> "To anyone who has practiced meditation or yoga; the word MANTRA is familiar as a word of power concentrated upon in meditation."

This explanation goes on to describe the most powerful Mantra in Hinduism. It continues:

> "The most important word of power in the Hindu scriptures is the word *OM*, which pronounced AUM means 'God', 'All', 'Being', 'The Answer'. Thought or intentness on its meaning will cause the exclusion of all other thought, ultimately bringing about the STATE of mind to which the meditator aspires."

At this time in their spiritual quest, the Moody Blues obviously believed deeply in this mantra because the last song on the album, "In Search of the Lost Chord", simply entitled "OM", has them actually chanting this Hindu Mantra for their listeners.

The *OM* can also be depicted, as it is in the case of the yantra, in a visual way. This also has a deep meaning because in the Hindu concept of reality everything vibrates at a particular rate thereby producing specific positive or negative KARMIC results. The visual depiction of the OM therefore is equally as powerful as the chant. The symbol for the OM is something very familiar to me because for about twelve years I wore one on a silver medallion around my neck. If you look at the figure on the opposite page top left hand corner you will see a picture of the *OM* symbol taken from the book The Tantric Way. It also seems to be a popular symbol to at least two well known Rock & Roll musicians. Looking at the picture on the opposite page once again, you not only see it on the cover of George Harrison's "Dark Horse" album, but you will also see it in the middle of Robert Plant's sweater. The word OM can be seen as well on the back of the Jimi Hendrix "Rainbow Bridge" album cover.

Even though the Moodies, as their admirers call them, exhibited a deep Hindu influence on their third album, the connection didn't end there. On the majority of their recordings Eastern religious ideals and concepts are present.

The fourth album entitled, "On the Threshold of a Dream", released in 1969, is less spiritual in its message; but once again "love" is presented as the answer to all the problems of life. One song after another uses the word *love* in its lyrical imagery, however, in the song "Have You Heard", a subtle reference to the Hindu mantra *OM* may once again be evident. One verse says:

> "Now you know that you are real
> Show your friends that you and me
> Belong to the same world
> Turned on to the same **WORD**
> Have you heard?"

Their next musical offering, also released in 1969, called "To Our Children's Children's Children", has them returning to their LSD inspired, New Age/Hindu ideology once again. Interspersed among their other lyrics are these lines:

The seed-syllable Oṃ.

Upper left: The visible Sanskrit representation of the Hindu Mantra OM taken from the book "The Tantric Way." Upper right: Robert Plant, one time lead vocalist for Led Zeppelin displaying the OM symbol on his sweatshirt. He has produced two solo albums recently entitled "Now and Zen" and "Manic Nirvana", both titles demonstrating an Eastern mystical connection Lower left: George Harrison - back cover of Dark Horse album. Lower right: Close up of OM symbol from Dark Horse album cover.

"Then everything will be as you will see *IN THE LIGHT*"

"Now that we're out here open your heart
To the universe of which we're a part"

"See with your mind, *leave your body behind*"

"Waiting for *rebirth*"

As well as:

"You've got to make the journey *out and in*"

The last line you just read is a clear reference to the Hindu concept of *pantheism*. **All is one**; either looking without or looking within. Everything is represented as *part of the WHOLE*. So as you can see, with the examples we have just given, the Hindu beliefs of reincarnation, pantheism, the Christ-within, and astral projection have been consistantly presented in the music of this group.

The fifth Moody Blues album released the following year continued the "love" theme. However, the album title, "A Question of Balance", once again revealed a foundation of Eastern Mysticism. The concept of balance: good and evil, male and female, YIN AND YANG, is called *Taoism*. In the song called "The Balance", the Moody Blues once again musically fantasize that man can achieve enlightenment by his own design. The song has almost a meditative aspect hidden within its lyrics. It says:

"And he asked, and he saw the tree above him,
And the stars,
And the veins in the leaf,
And the light, and the balance.
Whereon he thought of himself in balance...
And he knew he was.
Just open your eyes, and realize,
THE WAY ITS ALWAYS BEEN"

The *LIGHT*, the *BALANCE*, and *SELF-REALIZATION* are truly topics of Eastern origin and thought.

Though I have no doubt as I read the lyrics to their songs, they were possessed by a sincere desire to see love, peaceful co- existence, and harmony in this world, they were, nevertheless, being used by the Dragon to communicate *HIS* New Age gospel.

Their sixth album entitled, "Every Good Boy Deserves Favor", is a return to the more basic Hindu concept of reincarnation. The album starts with a cut called "Procession", which is basically a dramatized audio chronology of their interpretation of the theory of evolution.

The song, "After You Came", however, leaves no mystery as far as its teaching of the Hindu concept of the cycles of life, death, and rebirth. Hinduism teaches that we are all part of the great ocean of life which is "God". At our first birth, represented as a drop of water separated from the ocean, we become aware of this separateness and obtain an individual ego. We spend sometimes millions of evolutionary lifetimes as inanimate objects, plants, animals, and a multitude of human incarnations working our way back into the ocean where our individual ego and life will be once again comsumed and absorbed into the vast nothingness of eternity. Do the lyrics of this aforementioned song convey this message? You be the judge:

> "For some short time for a while you and I
> Were joined to eternity
> Then *we split in two back to me and you*
> Like the *rain rising from the sea*"

The New Age theme is completed on the last song of the album with the lines promoting extraterrestrials and globalism. They sing:

> "Where did I find all of these words
> Something inside me is burning
> There's life in other worlds
> **Maybe they'll come to earth**
> Helping man to find a way...
> One day I hope we'll be in perfect harmony
> **A planet with ONE MIND**"

On the album cover, a mystical looking old sage dangles a glowing crystal before the eyes of a fascinated young boy who has chosen this occult gift above the flowers and toys offered him by his friends. The CRYSTAL POWER craze that is sweeping America is obviously not new. The Moody Blues were promoting the same thing all the way back in 1971.

As I mentioned at the beginning of this section on Rock & Roll and the New Age Movement, it is clear the Moody Blues truly are the forefathers of the New Age in Rock & Roll. Though many of their compositions are love songs, within the framework of their music they still manage to get the message of the New Age across to their fans.

Their latest musical efforts produced within the last decade have not received the same acclaim which was generated during their early years. Perhaps that is because the time of their usefulness to the Dragon's cause has gradually come to an end. However, at least one or two songs from their latest material continue to reflect New Age/Hindu roots.

In 1981, they released their eighth album entitled, "Long Distance Voyager". The opening track called "The Voice", written by guitarist Justin Hayward, has them suggesting that their audience listen to the "VOICE WITHIN". Hayward writes:

> "Make a promise take a vow
> And trust your feelings
> It's easy now
> Understand the **VOICE within**
> And feel the changes already begin"

This refers to the "inner voice" that those of the New Age Movement have unfortunately come to know and trust. Sadly, it is "the voice" of deception.

In 1983, they released another album entitled, "The Present". It seems with this recording some of their initial power may have returned. The reason for this comment is a song on the album entitled "I Am". In it vocalist Ray Thomas, veteran "Moody" sings:

> "I am

I am
I am the son
Yes I am
I am the son
Yes, I am the son of love
I am"

Unfortunately, this claim is also false. There is only one true Son of Love.

The "I AM" concept portrayed in this song, also expressed in the similar verbal affirmation "I AM GOD", is a prime New Age teaching. Both of these statements mean the same thing. The "I AM" teaching is a doctrine taught by many New Age leaders such as Elizabeth Claire Prophet, the head of The Church Universal and Triumphant. This cult has borrowed their teachings from the same "ascended masters" who instructed Theosophists Madame Helena Petrovna Blavatsky and Alice Bailey; and to put it in a more contemporary light, New Age leaders such as Barbara Marx Hubbard and David Spangler.

Sadly, all of these people, including Ray Thomas, have bought into the same lie. The only person on earth who has ever legitimately claimed the right to say "I AM" was, and still is, the Lord Jesus Christ. He told the religious leaders of his day, "*Before Abraham* [the ancestral father of both Arabs and Jews] *was I AM*". Only Jesus is eternal for He is the Creator. He existed before anything. This is explained in Colossians 1:16-18.

In their next offering entitled, "The Other Side of Life", is a song called "The Spirit". The Moodies sing:

"Just keep looking don't be afraid
In the eye on the mind
I'm everywhere and yours to find
I'm not far just discover
I'm in you for I am love"

Many of the songs recorded by the Moody Blues are about "love". I only hope and pray that they soon come to realize only **God** is love. He is the ONLY ONE who can create in us TRUE love.

From the beginning to the present, including their latest "KEYS TO THE KINGDOM," a definite biblical reference, album after album, the Moody Blues, these long distance voyagers, have floundered in the depths of a deep and dark New Age sea. I pray with all my heart they eventually climb aboard God's life raft: the CROSS OF CHRIST.

Many more musicians sympathetic to the New Age agenda are surfacing today within the music world. Recent newcomers, Tuck and Patti, who received much of their initial recognition by remaking two Jimi Hendrix classics, "Little Wing", and "Castles Made of Sand", have another song on their debut album, "Love Warriors", which also shines brightly with the "white light" of New Age doctrine. The cut entitled, "Hold Out, Hold Up, And Hold On", finds vocalist Patti Cathcart singing the line, *"light to guide us it's INSIDE US"*. Finding the "light" inside us is a foundational New Age teaching.

Another recent new comer, Lenny Kravitz (whom *SPIN* magazine calls the Jesus of the hippies), is one more New Age enthusiast to look toward "love" for all the answers. His hit song, "Let Love Rule", however, sounds suspiciously like a resurrection of the Beatles hit, "Hey Jude".

The group Tears for Fears has produced a video of their song, "Sowing the Seeds of Love", which is so full of occult imagery (the all-seeing eye of Horus in the triangle, the pyramid, the Egyptian Ankh, astral travel, symbols of sun worship, etc.) that they could probably use it to teach a quick course in New Age, GLOBAL MINDED theology.

All in all it seems that contemporary Rock & Roll has chosen to embrace the New Age Movement with a bear hug.

Here are just a few more examples.

WHITE LION

One of the newest and most popular rock bands in the business is a band called White Lion. Their first hit single was a ballad entitled, "When The Children Cry". The words to this song could easily place them in the category of New Age sympathizers. Here are some of their lyrics:

> "No more PRESIDENTS
> And all the wars will end
> ONE UNITED WORLD
> UNDER GOD"

When lead vocalist Mike Tramp sings these words, what he is actually calling for is the implementation of one of the primary goals of the New Age agenda: The election of A ONE WORLD LEADER ("No more presidents"); the formation of A ONE WORLD GOVERNMENT ("One united world"); and the synthesis of A ONE WORLD RELIGION ("Under God").

God has already warned us in the Book of Revelation that this "United World" consciousness would come to prominence when the anti-Christ would take temporary control of the earth (Rev. 13:1-8). White Lion is either knowingly or unknowingly indoctrinating hundreds of thousands of their followers to accept the anti-Christ system of a *one world consciousness* as the will of GOD.

They couldn't be more wrong.

Another musician to call out for a *one world religion* is a man named Midge Ure. In his song, "Dear God", he sings, "Give me a WORLD-WIDE RELIGION".

ARE WE THE WORLD??

Archangel Michael, as some of his friends have dubbed Michael Jackson, though he may not even realize it, has assumed a position as an acolyte for the anti-Christ. Michael Jackson's song, "We Are The World", has been adopted as the anthem for global consciousness. In the song is a line which says, "As God has shown us by turning stones to bread". Obviously, the spirits who helped him to write his New Age masterpiece must have had a lapse of memory. Turning stones into bread was exactly what Jesus *REFUSED* to do during his spiritual battle with the Devil in the Judean wilderness at the beginning of his three year ministry (Matt. 4:1-11). Jesus told Satan, *"Man does not live by bread alone, but by every word that proceedeth out of the mouth of God."* That, Jesus declared, was *HIS* bread!

Also, quite contrary to the declaration, "We Are The World", which is the main theme of the song recorded by Michael Jackson and his musical colleagues, the Bible has something quite different to say about how we are to perceive our lives on this Earth.

Jesus said if you are going to follow Him you will be just the *opposite* of the world. His WORD on this matter is crystal clear. He says of His disciples:

> *"They are NOT OF THIS WORLD even as I AM NOT OF THIS WORLD."*
>
> Jesus Christ - John 17:16

Christians are to be *IN* the world but not *OF* the world; a truth Michael Jackson and his friends have yet to discover.

THE NERO SYNDROME

Rock & Roll musicians seem to be more aware of environmental problems today than ever before. As a result of this heightened awareness, environmental issues are becoming paramount to the musical New Age agenda; but as with every other problem facing humanity, there has to be a cause. In this case, the old saying, "When in Rome, do as the Romans do", seems to be quite apropos. Since a cause must be found for the environmental problems facing the planet, why not, as Nero did in Rome, blame it on the Christians? Well, that is precisely what the New Age Movement is attempting to do.

I know, right about now you're probably thinking, 'Oh come on now, can you prove that ridiculous statement??' As a matter of fact...I CAN.

In *TIME* magazine January 2, 1989, the issue entitled, "Planet of the Year", a hypothesis is proposed identifying the source of all the global environmental problems that face our world today. The hypothesis put forth in *TIME* is nothing short of absurd, but here is what it states in the article entitled, "What On Earth Are We Doing":

> "Humanity's current predatory relationship with nature reflects a man-centered world view that has evolved over the ages. Almost every society has had its myths about the earth and its origins...In many pagan societies, the earth was seen as a mother, a fertile giver of life. Nature -- the soil, forest, sea -- was endowed with divinity, and mortals were sub-ordinate to it." [Worship of the earth as a

BEING and a MOTHER is known in New Age jargon as the GAIA hypothesis.]

That is just the beginning of the quote. Now here comes what I call the "Nero Syndrome" (Nero blamed the Christians for burning Rome). The sentiment expressed in *TIME* draws an obvious parallel. The article goes on to say:

"The JUDEO-CHRISTIAN tradition introduced a radically different concept. The earth was the creation of a monotheistic God, who, after shaping it, ordered its inhabitants, in the words of GENESIS: 'Be fruitful and multiply, and replenish the earth and subdue it: and have dominion over the fish of the sea and over the fowl of the air and over every living thing that moveth upon the earth.' The idea of dominion [now get this part!] could be interpreted as an *invitation to use nature as a convenience. THUS THE SPREAD OF CHRISTIANITY*, which is generally considered to have paved the way for the development of TECHNOLOGY, may at the same time have CARRIED THE SEEDS OF THE *WANTON EXPLOITATION OF NATURE* that often accompanied technical progress."[5]

Now, if you stop for just a minute and analyze what you just read, you can't help but conclude that there is a subtle message being proclaimed to the readers of *TIME* magazine. What is this message? Simply this: The pagan religions of the past had more respect for the earth and were more ecologically beneficial to man than Christianity. The spread of Christianity, more precisely, the Judeo-Christian ethic, is, according to this obviously New Age propagandist article, actually to blame for the environmental problems of the earth! Somehow Christians have caused all these ecological disasters by our "wanton exploitation of nature". That, in a nut shell, is what this article implies.

Well, if you don't mind a quick aside from the topic of New Age music for just a minute, I would like to answer these charges made by *TIME*, if I may, with just a brief word to *All* the Christianity bashing New Agers, whoever and wherever they may be.

It seems a bit ridiculous to try to blame all the ecological problems we are facing in our world today on the Christians. If you read Genesis 1:28, the scripture verse which was quoted in the *TIME* magazine article, a little more *carefully*, you will notice it says SUBDUE the Earth, *NOT ABUSE* it. According to a *proper* interpretation of the Bible, God, who by the way was the first person to teach the agricultural advantages of crop rotation (Ex. 23:10,11), tells us we are *ALL* to care for the Earth He has given us, and TRUE Christians do. True Christians love and care for *ALL* God's creation. That includes the planet on which we live.

If man would just follow the laws that God has given us (I might quickly add, totally for our *benefit*), and stop our sin, the earth, as well as its inhabitants wouldn't have all these problems. Unfortunately that will only happen when the Lord Jesus Christ personally and **PHYSICALLY RETURNS TO EARTH**. Intelligent people should easily see the absurdity in making Christianity a scapegoat for world environmental problems. It is quite obvious that pure spiritual ignorance and the demonically inspired depravity of the human condition is the more logical ecological villain.

As we have continued to evidence throughout this book, Rock & Roll musicians worldwide, many of them sympathetic to New Age ideologies, are not the slightest bit hesitant to join the rest of the New Age in their condemnation of biblical Christianity.

There are a lot more examples I could have given of other Rock & Roll groups equally sypathetic to the messages of the New Age Movement, but now let's shift our attention to the flip side of the musical New Age coin.

NEW AGE MUSIC

Even though, as we have just shown you, some Rock & Roll, evidenced by the message it communicates to its audience, is undeniably New Age music, there is another style of music more familiar to most New Agers which has adopted the moniker "New Age Music" as its own. It is that airy, etheric, mesmerizing, trance-inducing music that we briefly mentioned at the beginning of this chapter.

All around the world there is a growing movement of New Age musicians. Some of them play nothing but instrumental music, such as harpist Andreas Vollenweider, saxophonist Paul Winter, and keyboardists Stephen Halpern and Kitaro; a few others, such as Nicki Skully and Constance Demby, have New Age lyrics to accompany some of their songs. There are hundreds of musicians that fit into these categories. Some have come to greater prominence in New Age circles than others. The following person is just one example of a New Age musician that has clearly been touched by the deeper spiritual darkness of New Age music.

CUMBEY vs. DEMBY

No chapter on the New Age, music or otherwise, would be complete without at least mentioning one of pioneers of the exposition of this phenomenon called the New Age Movement. The person of whom I speak is trial lawyer, lecturer, and anti-New Age activist Constance Cumbey. In the early 1980's, she received much acclaim in the Christian world for her excellent work entitled, The Hidden Dangers of the Rainbow, which remains a classic to this day. Many sincere, but sincerely *wrong* New Agers have been challenged, changed, and converted to Jesus Christ as a result of reading this informative and enlightening book.

Constance Cumbey is a devoted Christian, and for many years has remained a staunch opponent of the New Age Movement.

There is another Constance, however, who is a direct antithesis of Mrs. Cumbey. Her name is Demby. She is not a daughter of the Deity, but sadly, she is a New Age daughter of the Dragon.

MUSICAL CHANNEL - CONSTANCE DEMBY

The Bible says in I Tim. 4:1:

> *"...that in the latter times some shall depart from the faith, giving heed to SEDUCING SPIRITS and DOCTRINES OF DEVILS..."*

Though you may have believed that all the knowledge you have been taught in this world has originated in the mind of man, I would like you to understand that, as this scripture you just read declares, there are many teachings that have come to mankind via the mouths of devils. They can and do TEACH. You can also be sure whatever it is they are teaching, if followed, will ultimately lead a person further away from God. Reincarnation, astral projection, sorcery, Transcendental Meditation, Yoga, individual Godhood, Christ consciousness, self-realization, and witchcraft, to name but a few are perfect examples of the teachings, or "DOCTRINES of devils". As we have mentioned earlier, these spirits have taught their doctrines most effectively by using men and women to record their ideas in literature, and more recently, through advanced technology on audio and video tape. But demons not only teach; they also make **personal appearances!**

A chosen person is able to receive information from a spirit and is prompted, or in some cases forced to share that knowledge with others. However, some people also have the capability of becoming the vehicle for the spirit to **speak through** and literally possess. In the New Age Movement this supernatural phenomenon is called *CHANNELING.*

Channeling is allowing a spirit to enter one's body for the express purpose of communicating or disseminating information to another person or a group. Channeling is practiced by such New Age personalities as: J.Z. Knight (channeling Ramtha), Jach Percel (channeling a spirit calling itself Lazaris) and Kevin Ryerson, of Shirley MacLaine fame (channeling entities: Tom McPherson and John). Many disincarnate spirits, with names such as: RAMTHA, LAZARIS, MAFU, JESUS OF THE LIGHT, TOM McPHERSON, SETH, and others too numerous to mention use the vocal cords of their host bodies to TEACH! The channelers may call this channeling, but the Bible calls this same spiritual phenomena something different...DEMONIC POSSESSION!

New Age musician Constance Demby is also familiar with channeling, but in a rather unique way -- *musically*. She says that the New Age space music she plays is actually channeled through her by spirit entities from outer space. She is in essence claiming to be a musical *channel* for these spirits.

However, there is another aspect to her channeling experiences that is even more intriguing. These "alien" beings have also channeled music *directly into her recording equipment!*

In a New Age magazine called *Connecting Link*, which deals basically with the channeling phenomena, is an interview with Constance Demby in which she relates some very unusual incidents of channeling, which she recalls as being among the most memorable of those she has experienced. One of them, as we just mentioned, involved the direct channeling of music into her recording equipment. Demby recalls:

> "Starting Dec. 20, 1987, I began receiving a series of signals from outer space that came directly through the recording equipment in my studio. It was a series of tones unlike anything I've ever heard on earth...The tones have very unusual harmonic and rhythmic patterns that you know are not from this plane of existence."[6]

In the same *Connecting Link* article, she also remembers one very special concert she performed at the Alaron Center in Sausalito, California, on October 1, 1983. Why does she consider this concert to have been such a special one? Let's let her tell us in her own words:

> "There was a very unusual, very special potent feel in the concert hall that night, and all of the hundreds of people there were completely transfixed. We became totally out of time. I thought I had played about one hour and a half and it was actually three hours. It was the most I have ever experienced being OVER-SHADOWED BY *SPIRITUAL ENTITIES*, WHICH PEOPLE SAW IN THE ROOM AND *SURROUNDING ME*. Alaron has a very palpable feeling of *CHANNELING*."[7]

Though Constance Demby feels that the music she produces emanates from a higher plane of existence, it is clear by reading a few of her song titles that, surprisingly enough, a deep Hindu influence is once again at work. This observation becomes even more apparent when you read the dedication printed on the paper insert contained within the cassette case of her Alaron concert tape. It says, "Music composed, performed and produced by Constance Demby -- Dedicated to SANT AJAIB SINGH JI". Ajaib Singh is a guru from India. "SANT" means saint, and "JI" is a Hindu suffix denoting great respect.

One particular instrumental song on the Alaron tape entitled, "Guru Dev Aja", includes an explanation for the purpose of the song. It is actually a musical mantra or meditation, which could properly be defined as a prayer. This musical prayer is also an invocation. Constance Demby explains the purpose for the song. She says: "This is an invitation for the *radiant form* of the Master (Guru Dev) to appear within (Aja)."

Simply translated, this is a request for the powerful spirits who control her guru SANT AJAIB SINGH, whom she calls her God (Guru Dev literally means DIVINE MASTER) to enter into and totally possess her. Her music, beautiful and entrancing as it may be, is nevertheless just one more beat of the Dragon's heart.

NEW AGE WINTER

Another popular and very well known New Age musician is Paul Winter. His first album entitled, "Icarus", recorded with his band, the Paul Winter Consort, is considered to be a classic in the realms of New Age Music. However, one thing I discovered about this album clearly supports the premise we have been establishing throughout this book. It astonished me to find out that the first Paul Winter Consort album was produced by a man named George Martin. For those not familiar with the name, he was also the producer of a group we spoke of earlier...The Beatles! Martin said, however, the album "Icarus" by Paul Winter was "The finest album I ever made". It is evident that even the **producer** of the Beatles obviously has a key part to play in the Dragon's master plan.

Paul Winter not only has his band behind him, but he also uses the actual sounds and calls of animals on his recordings. He has literally married his music to nature, or in a very real way to the earth itself. This, however, is not at all surprising considering the title of one of his albums, "Missa GAIA/Earth Mass".

Remember, as we mentioned earlier, Gaia is the name given to the "goddess" or "Mother Earth" so popular in Witchcraft and the New Age Movement today. To call the earth Gaia, is to allude to the fact that the earth is not just a planet -- but rather a living being with a living soul. In the New Age Movement, the planet Earth is worshiped as our Mother. This worship of the earth is actually a carryover from many ancient pagan cultures.

Earth worship is considered by the God of the Bible to be idolatry. The Bible says in the past people "*...worshipped and served the creature [or creation] MORE than the Creator...*" (Romans 1:25). Mother Earth or Gaia is a pagan concept totally condemned by God; but promoted and embraced by New Age musician Paul Winter.

Winter also recorded part of another album entitled, "Canyon", in the Episcopal Cathedral of ST. JOHN THE DIVINE in New York City. In May of 1984, this same New Age church unveiled, and for many days publicly displayed, a new form of the crucifix called a **"Christa"** which, instead of Jesus, revealed a *FEMINIZED* bare-breasted "Christ" on the cross -- another powerful symbol of goddess worship. That action, however, to those who are familiar with this New Age cathedral, should not come as a surprise, for this is the same church that invited the cast from the Broadway, tribal musical, "HAIR", to perform their "Aquarian Age" songs of blasphemy and perversion within its "hallowed halls". They named the resultant recording "Divine Hair".

The Cathedral of St. John the Divine has also provided a platform for some of the most well known and powerful New Age leaders in the world today, such as David Spangler (advocate of a *LUCIFERIC* initiation), who fully support and defend the Gaia hypothesis. This is the church where Paul Winter chose to record his music. So as you can clearly see by his songs, his beliefs, and his professional and spiritual associations that paganism, blasphemy, idolatry, witchcraft, and of course Hinduism, are the collective nutrients that give life to the New Age music of Paul Winter.

Though I do not deny the beauty and wonder contained within nature, there is one major difference between myself and these New Age musicians. I do not worship the Earth...I worship its CREATOR, Jesus Christ. The Bible states very clearly in the Book of Colossians, Chapter 1 verse 16:

"For BY HIM were ALL THINGS created, that are in heaven, and that are in earth, visible and invisible, whether they be thrones, or

dominions, or principalities, or powers: ALL THINGS were cre-
ated BY HIM AND FOR HIM."

Now here is another obvious tie with the Dragon: the *refusal* to worship Jesus Christ. Is the spirit behind the New Age Movement and its music and the spirit behind Rock & Roll any different? Not in the slightest. You can argue all you wish about the destructive lyrical content in Rock & Roll songs, but as you can see, in the case of New Age music, the Dragon doesn't need lyrics at all to get the job done. Sadly, music, such as I have been discussing in this chapter, is being produced by people who, once again, have surrendered their wills to the purpose of the Dragon. Even though most of this New Age music is purely instrumental, with or without lyrics, it is nevertheless spiritually destructive to the human soul.

Neither time nor space permits the individual mention of the hundreds of New Age musicians in the world today and the detrimental effects that their music has produced in many lives. One consequence, however, appears rather consistent in the cases we have researched. The people involved with this New Age music, both musicians and their listeners, have found themselves involuntarily entering into trance states where contact with spirit entities frequently occurred. Eventually these people became, just as the shamans and yogis, **controlled** by these spirits. In a vast number of cases this ultimately destroyed their lives. The only way many of them found escape from the grasp of these powerful seducing spirits was to surrender their lives to JESUS CHRIST.

New Age radio stations, which not only constantly play this type of music, but also have on-air meditation as well as "channeling" sessions, are popping up all over America. They have quite literally become catalysts for a global mass possession.

These extremely intelligent and yet inconceivably diabolical spirits who are the ones behind the production of this music are even now, as you read this book, influencing, seducing, controlling, and in many cases possessing many of your friends and neighbors; and perhaps even family members, who, when the time comes, because of their *pre-programming,* will be totally unable to resist the power and will of the anti-Christ. They will quite literally become, as Mötley Crüe sings, "children of the Beast".

We are truly living in the last days of time on Earth as we know it. Jesus Christ is soon going to return to this planet Earth to rescue it and redeem the inhabitants (who have been obedient to His WORD). Hebrews 5:9 states:

"And being made perfect, He became the author of eternal salvation unto all them that obey Him..."

Jesus will then establish a millenium of righteousness and peace, the likes of which were only experienced by Adam and his immediate descendants at the dawn of creation.

That is good news indeed.

There is, however, some very bad news, as well. Before the reign of peace is established, many of the people on earth will be the recipients of a merciless attack perpetrated by the Dragon and his minions to bring destruction and death to the inhabitants of this planet. The entire earth and its population will be virtually devastated by every device and design of darkness that the Dragon can deliver.

The soon coming world leader, the "man of peace", will not, I repeat, WILL *NOT* be the *TRUE CHRIST*. He will be Anti-Christ, and, yes, he will be using that infamous number, "666", as his very own; but this should not actually be surprising. The New Age Movement already considers this a very sacred number and highly recommends its use as frequently as possible. The use of the "666", and its many adaptations, they say, will increase the positive vibrations of the planet. They are very WRONG, but that, as they say, is another story.

The "global consciousness" initiative that is currently underway, spearheading events such as Earth Day, the Harmonic Convergence, etc., so strongly promoted by the spiritually ignorant Rock & Roll musicians of this world, is just the open door of opportunity that Anti-Christ needs. In order to have a "one world leader" the world must be of one mind, or to put in a New Age vernacular, we must adopt a "GLOBAL CONSCIOUSNESS".

The U.S.A. for Africa/"We Are The World" event -- the musical glasnost called The Moscow Peace Festival -- Live Aid -- Farm Aid I-V -- and yes, even "innocent" Woodstock have become the true harbingers of a New Age, not one of light, but one of unparalleled darkness.

After it begins, it will only last a short span of seven years, but during that time the annihilation and carnage on this planet will reach proportions never even imagined by any man or woman alive on Earth today. It will be a time of such devastation that if Jesus Christ did not come back and personally intervene, there would be nothing left of life on Earth; and for the first time in the history of the world (due to the advent of nuclear weaponry) this is now a distinct possibility.

The Bible says, however, that Jesus will indeed return, put an end to the destruction, and remove those who perpetuate death and war into eternal JUDGMENT (Rev. 11:18). You might not like those facts if you happen to be involved in Satanism, Witchcraft, Voodoo, Channeling, Goddess Worship, Tantric Yoga, TM, Astral Projection, Sorcery, Spiritism, New Age Music, Rock & Roll, or any number of other occult practices promoted by the *New Agers* and their Luciferic brand of spirituality; but **those are the facts.** Regardless of the concerted effort put forth by the Dragon and his greatly deceived followers, he will ultimately **LOSE THE FINAL WAR!**

CHAPTER 14

FROM DARKNESS TO LIGHT

"to open their eyes and turn them from darkness to light and from the power of Satan unto God..."

Acts 26:18

Since I began the research for this book, my eyes have continually been opened by the Holy Spirit (I give Him *all* the credit) to understand the Dragon's plan in progress. I will now share with you some of what the LORD has shown me concerning these revelations.

As more and more darkness manifests itself on the Earth, people will become more and more *immune* to evil. Their senses will be numbed and cauterized as they repetitively ingest images of darkness continually displayed before their eyes through cinema, video, and television; images created by a demon inspired humanity. The general public is even now being conditioned to apathetically accept atrocities of violence, murder, blood sacrifice, and perversion of every sort, interpreting such actions not as *good* or *evil,* but instead, being coerced into viewing this behavior as a matter of personal choice.

Left-handed black tantric Hinduism, Shamanism, Satanism, Voodoo, Witchcraft, Santeria, and yes, even Rock & Roll also reject the concept of absolute good or evil. Everything is relative to the experience. Satan's goal is the reconditioning of the morals of society. The plan is the induction of the population into a tolerance of deviant behavior, while their consciences atrophy. His desire is to create an *AMORAL* society steeped in demonic activity: one that will bow to the anti-Christ; whether he comes in peace, as he will in his inauguration; or in war, as he will when he begins to show his *TRUE* colors. People all over the globe are even now being prepared for the Dragon's ultimate deception; the one that, if and when they accept it, will cost them their eternal lives.

No matter what *you* want to do with this planet, *Satan* wants to **destroy** it. You say you don't believe in the Devil? -- that suits him just fine. Just because you don't believe he exists, won't make him go away. He will be a permanent resident of the earth until his final defeat and banishment into the "Lake of Fire". The Bible calls him "the **Destroyer**", and that will be his major preoccupation until that final day.

To deal with the Dragon is one of the main reasons that Jesus Christ is going to return to this Earth: He will manifest to all peoples everywhere the GLORY of His power and...**FINISH THE WAR** that began almost 2000 years ago. The Bible states:

> *"For this purpose the Son of God was manifested that he might destroy the works of the devil."*
>
> 1 JOHN 4:8

Jesus loves all people, and His substitutionary death, or **vicarious atonement** (a concept extremely upsetting to many New Age leaders and their disciples) will work for anyone who is willing to utilize it. But I also am obligated by God to show you two Bible scriptures that might open your eyes to another side of this loving Jesus. TRUE, He does love us; but He will also be the one to *JUDGE* and *EVALUATE* the life of every person who has ever been born. To those who hate, murder, lie, steal, and destroy; to the drug dealers, abortionists, sexual deviates, spouse and child abusers, sorcerers, ROCK & ROLL rebels, and God haters, I have but one word for you - REPENT! If you do not, I have another word for you - BEWARE!

When most people think of Jesus Christ, they imagine Him as He is portrayed in many religious pictures: a brown haired, bearded man with sandal shod feet, a lamb around His neck, and a staff in His hand. They envision a passive and peaceful man: the one who allowed himself to be degraded, spat upon, beaten, mocked, ridiculed, and finally, nailed to a Roman cross. The first time He came to earth that is exactly who He was and what He endured. When He comes back, however, to bring **judgment** on the evils of this world, it will be a much different story. The *REAL* Jesus Christ (*NOT* the New Age, ascended master, **IMPOSTOR** Jesus: the non-judgmental one portrayed in all this God-cursed esoteric, NON-BIBLICAL literature such as The Aquarian Gospel of Jesus the Christ, the Gnostic Gospels, The Lost Books of the Bible, the Urantia Book, etc.) does love everyone, but He also **HATES SIN!** It has destroyed His universe and corrupted His creatures and will be **ERADICATED!** The next time you think about the "gentle" Jesus, consider these scriptures as well:

> *"...the Lord Jesus shall be revealed from Heaven with His mighty angels, in flaming fire **taking vengeance** on them that know not God, and that **obey not** the gospel of our Lord Jesus Christ: Who shall be punished with everlasting destruction from the presence of the Lord, and from the glory of His power..."*
>
> II Thes. 1:7-9

And for those who would destroy His creatures or creation:

> *"And the nations were angry, and thy <u>wrath</u> is come, and the time of the dead that they should be **judged**, and that thou shouldest give reward unto thy servants the prophets and to the saints, and them that fear thy name small and great; and shouldest **DESTROY** them which destroy the earth."*
>
> Revelation 11:18

Yes, my friends, Jesus will be returning **SOON** to straighten up this mess that humanity, with the Dragon's help, has produced. He will return in the sky at the Battle of *Armageddon.* The Bible says:

> *"And I saw heaven opened, and behold a white horse; and he that sat upon him was called Faithful and True, and in righteousness he doth **judge** and **make war**. His eyes were as a flame of fire, and on his head were many crowns; and he had a name written, that no man knew, but he himself. And he was clothed with a vesture dipped in blood: and **his name is called THE WORD OF GOD**. And the armies which were in heaven followed him upon white horses, clothed in fine linen, white and clean. And out of his mouth goeth a sharp sword, that with it he should smite the nations: and he shall rule them with a rod of iron: and he treadeth the winepress*

*of the fierceness and wrath of Almighty God. And he hath on his vesture and on his thigh a name written, **KING OF KINGS, AND LORD OF LORDS**."*

Revelation 19:11-16

ROCK & ROLLERS, NEW AGERS, SATANISTS, SORCERERS, SHA-MANS, WITCHES, OCCULTISTS, ATHEISTS, YOGIS, FALSE RELIGIONISTS, and PLEASURE LOVERS; THIS IS NOT A FANTASY - IT IS A **FACT**! **JUDGMENT DAY IS COMING**, but *YOU* can avoid it. There is still hope for you. Read on.

CONCLUSION

I did not have the space to go into very much detail or reveal some of the other incredible information that we have uncovered in our research. Hopefully, that will soon be made available as well, but I hope and pray you can now understand at least part of the plan behind ROCK & ROLL. The life, the power, the energy, and the SPIRIT that produces it is the enemy of all souls.

Having been a musician and lead vocalist, who at one time in my life lived and breathed the Rock & Roll existence, 15 years worth, I am sad to say I have witnessed the Dragon win many to his lifestyle with his Rock & Roll HEART-BEAT. Even to this day, when I think of JIMI, JANIS, JIM, JOHN, BRIAN, KEITH, and the multitudes of others who have fallen victim on the Dragon's battlefield of souls, I am still greatly grieved and saddened. The realization that I can do nothing for these who are even now experiencing a CHRISTLESS *ETERNITY* sometimes produces in me such overwhelming despair that all I can do is weep. I weep for these souls who can no longer be affected by the information that you have just read, and I weep for the ones who will ignore this warning and die without accepting Jesus Christ as Savior.

My partner in the Christian Militia, Ray Delaforce, Christian friend, brother, and dedicated researcher extraordinaire (May the LORD bless you my brother eternally for your tireless dedication to Him) and I have spent thousands of hours preparing this book for those who are still eligible to receive the eternal peace and freedom of which we are already partakers. This glorious life is *FREE FOR THE ASKING.*

Tragically, but truly, the Dragon's heart is one that beats in those who are his **slaves**, but I rejoice to tell you that there is another heartbeat that yearns to fill you with True Life and Power which will <u>SET YOU FREE</u>!. It belongs to the LORD JESUS CHRIST. He wants to bring His peace, love, and hope into *YOUR* life. He wants to remove the unholy spirits within you and fill you with the Holy Spirit.

I have personally fought with demon spirits many times myself so I know how real the battle can be. They have physically held me down on my bed in an attempt to frighten, and on occasion even seduce me. Their power over me, however, was broken over 1900 years ago at a place called Calvary. The only reason they left my room and freed me when they did was because I commanded them in the NAME OF JESUS CHRIST **TO GO!** I have that authority over these dark powers and principalities because I belong to **HIM. I have been bought with a price...HIS BLOOD.**

The Dragon is after *YOU* as well. He wants to destroy your life and capture your soul and spirit for eternity. Without Jesus Christ as your LORD AND SAVIOR you too will *LOSE* the war.

The reason I wrote this book is because I am a WINNER! No matter what past wrongs or sins you've committed in your life, God can MAKE YOU A WINNER TOO!!

You may be a Rock & Roll or New Age musician, a singer, a roadie, record producer, promoter, or a rock magazine publisher; a record store owner, a disc jockey, a radio station manager, or simply one of Rock & Roll's millions of fans already badly singed by the Dragon's fiery breath. You too can be *SET FREE* from the HEARTBEAT OF THE DRAGON...I can't think of a better time than RIGHT NOW.

It's time to put aside your pride and fear. Jesus Christ loves you and so do I. Make the transition from darkness to the true LIGHT right now. Open your heart to Him and receive eternal life. Pray this prayer and mean it with all your heart:

Heavenly Father,

I know that I am a sinner and I need your forgiveness. I have sinned against you. I invite Jesus Christ to be my Lord and Savior. I will no longer serve darkness and I will turn to the Light and live for Him. Jesus, thank you for dying on the cross for my sins and rising again to give me new Life. I give my life totally to you. Holy

Spirit, fill me now, use me for your will, and teach me all about God. I will serve you Lord as long as I live. Thank you Lord Jesus for saving me and making me born again. In Jesus' name I pray. Amen.

If you prayed that prayer and **really meant it,** you are now a child of the TRUE God. Please do these three things to help you in your walk with Him:

1. Turn away and separate yourself from anything that is sin. So what if you get ridiculed and laughed at by your "friends"! So did JESUS. Be assured, the wages of sin will always be DEATH. (Rom. 6:23)

2. Get a Bible and read it *every day*. God's Word will be your key source of life, hope, and change. Pray, and talk to God about anything that is on your mind. He is now your Father and will help you.

3. Find a good *BIBLE BELIEVING* church and attend services there at least once a week. Also try to find a good Bible study to attend where what you learn **agrees** with what the Bible teaches. **Correct** knowledge of the Bible will greatly strengthen your faith in God.

If we, here at the Christian Militia, can help you in any way or if you have any question, please feel free to call or write us at:

THE CHRISTIAN MILITIA
P.O. BOX 7017
STERLING HEIGHTS, MI 48311
OR CALL
(313)-247-8186

REMEMBER: The Dragon is a <u>MURDERER</u> and a <u>LIAR!!!</u>
JESUS CHRIST IS THE *PRINCE OF LIFE* AND *ETERNAL LORD*.
WHO WILL YOU SERVE???   THE CHOICE IS YOURS.
AMEN.

P.S. And Father...thank you for making this dream a reality. I love You.

GOD'S WORD
I John 2:15-18

"Love not the world, neither the things that are in the world. If any man love the world the love of the Father is not in him.

For all that is in the world, the lust of the flesh, and the lust of the eyes, and the pride of life, is not of the Father, but is of the world.

And the world will pass away, and the lust thereof; but whoever does the will of God will live forever.

*Little children, it is the last time; and as you have heard that anti-christ shall come, even now are there many anti-christs; whereby we know that it is **the last time.**"*

NOTES

CHAPTER 1 - AND THEY WORSHIPED THE DRAGON

CHAPTER 2 - THE SHAMAN'S DANCE

1. Danny Sugerman, *The Doors Illustrated History*, William Morrow and Company, 1983, p. 74

2. Jerry Hopkins/Danny Sugerman, *No One Here Gets Out Alive*, Warner Books, 1980, pp. 158-160

3. Mircea Eliade, *Yoga: Immortality and Freedom*, Princeton University Press, 1969, p. 338

4. Stephen Davis, *Hammer of the Gods: The Led Zeppelin Story*, Ballantine Books, 1985, p. 198

5. *USA Today*, Jan. 13, 1984, p. 5D

6. Tony Sanchez, *Up and Down with The Rolling Stones*, Signet Books, 1979, p. 45

7. Dan & Steve Peters, *Why Knock Rock*, Bethany House Publishers, 1984, p. 184

8. *Time*, June 3, 1967, p. 43

9. Dan & Steve Peters, *Why Knock Rock*, Bethany House Publishers, 1984, p. 185

10. Fletcher A. Brothers, *The Rock Report*, Starburst Publishers, 1987, p. 66

11. I.M. Lewis, *Ecstatic Religion: A Study of Shamanism and Spirit Possession*, Routledge, 1989, p. 51

12. *Rolling Stone*, September 4, 1980, pp. 10, 21, 23

13. Dave Hunt/T.A. McMahon, *America: The Sorcerers New Apprentice*, Harvest House, 1988, p. 245

14. Ibid., p. 240

15. *Creem*, March 1985, p. 64

CHAPTER 3 - TO POSSESS A RACE

1. *Rolling Stone*, February 12, 1976, p. 83

2. *Spin*, June 1989, p. 32

3. Ed Ward/Geoffrey Stokes/Ken Tucker, *Rock of Ages: The History of Rock & Roll*, Rolling Stone Press, 1986, p. 149

4. *Spin*, June 1989, p. 32

5. Ibid.

6. Charles White, *The Life and Times of Little Richard*, Harmony Books, 1984, pp. 119, 120

7. Ibid., p. 219

8. Ibid.

9. Ibid.

10. Ibid., p. 220

11. Ibid., p. 216

12. Ibid., p. 217

13. Ibid., pp. 71, 72

14. Ibid., pp. 205, 206

15. Jacob Aranza, *Backwards Masking Unmasked*, Huntington House Inc., 1983, p. 12

CHAPTER 4 - VOODOO CHILDREN

1. Alfred Metraux, *Voodoo in Haiti*, Shocken Books, 1972, p. 95

2. Wade Davis, *The Serpent and the Rainbow*, Warner Books, 1985, p. 329

3. *Spin*, April 1990, p. 98

4. Mircea Eliade, *Yoga: Immortality and Freedom*, Princeton University Press, 1969, p. 300

5. Veronica Ions, *Indian Mythology*, Hamlyn Publishing, 1967, p. 64

6. David Henderson, *'Scuse Me While I Kiss the Sky: The Life of Jimi Hendrix*, Bantam Books, 1983, p. 250

7. *Life*, October 3, 1969, p. 74

8. Dave Hunt/T.A. McMahon, *America: The Sorcerers New Apprentice*, Harvest House Publishers, 1988, p. 241

9. Soundtrack from the film *Jimi Hendrix*, interview with Alan Douglas (Side 4).

10. Ibid., Fayne Pridgon

11. David Henderson, *'Scuse Me While I Kiss the Sky: The life of Jimi Hendrix*, Bantam Books, 1983, p. 250

12. *Rolling Stone*, July 13-27, 1989, p. 78

13. Ibid.

14. Charles White, *The Life and Times of Little Richard*, Harmony Books, 1984, p. 197

CHAPTER 5 - MAD GODS AND ENGLISHMEN

1. *County Post Times Herald*, June 11, 1971, p. 22

2. Tal Brooke, *Riders of the Cosmic Circuit*, Lion Publishing Company, 1986, p. 202

3. Anton Szandor LaVey, *The Satanic Bible*, Avon Books, 1969, p. 30

4. Ibid.

5. Ibid., p. 31

CHAPTER 6 - THE MAGICAL MISERY TOUR

1. Dave Hunt/T.A. McMahon, *America: The Sorcerers New Apprentice*, Harvest House Publishers, 1988, p. 239

2. *Musician* (Special Collectors Edition - Beatles and Rolling Stones), 1988, p. 20

3. Dennis Corle, *The Pied Piper of Rock*, J.B. Printing Ministry, 1985, p. 98

4. Ibid.

5. Ibid.

6. Ibid.

7. Dan & Steve Peters, *Why Knock Rock*, Bethany House Publishers, 1984, p. 91

8. Jacob Aranza, *Backwards Masking Unmasked*, Huntington House Inc., 1983, p. 11

9. *Musician* (Special Collectors Edition - Beatles and Rolling Stones), 1988, p. 12

CHAPTER 7 - L.S.D. LOVE POTION #9

1. Rabi Maharaj, *Death of a Guru*, Harvest House Publishers, 1984, p. 75

2. *Rolling Stone*, October 22, 1987, p. 44

3. Eric Burdon, *I Used To Be An Animal, But I'm All Right Now*, Faber and Faber, 1986, pp. 149, 150

CHAPTER 8 - CHILDREN OF THE BEAST

1. Sandy Robertson, *The Aleister Crowley Scrapbook*, Samuel Weiser Inc., 1988. p. 11

2. Aleister Crowley, *The World's Tragedy*, Falcon Press, 1985, p. XXXIX

3. Ibid., p. XXXI

4. Aleister Crowley, *Magick In Theory and Practice*, Dover Publications, 1976, p. VII

5. Ibid., p. XXII

CHAPTER 9 - LED ZEPPELIN: STAIRWAY TO HADES

1. Aleister Crowley, *Magick In Theory and Practice*, Dover Publications, 1976, p. 39

2. Ibid.

3. Stephen Davis, *Hammer of the Gods: The Led Zeppelin Saga*, Ballantine Books, 1985, p. 134

CHAPTER 10 - TWINKLE TWINKLE EVIL STAR: THE LEGACY OF THE PENTAGRAM

1. Ted Schwartz/Duane Empey, *Satanism: Is Your Family Safe*, Zondervan Publishing House, 1988, p. 102

2. Constance Cumbey, *New Age Monitor*, June 1986, Vol. I, No. 2, p. 7

3. Ibid., pp. 7, 8

4. Ibid., p. 8

5. Ibid., p. 9

6. Dr. A.S. Raleigh, *Occult Geometry*, DeVorss & Co., 1981, p. 44

7. Ibid., p. 45

8. Anton Szandor LaVey, *The Satanic Bible*, Avon Books, 1969, p. 110

9. Ibid.

10. *Circus*, January 31, 1984, p. 70

11. *Rip*, December, 1990, p. 102

12. Marilyn Ferguson, *The Aquarian Conspiracy*, J.P. Tarcher, Inc., 1980, p. 79

13. Colin Wilson, *Aleister Crowley: The Nature of The Beast*, Aquarian Press, 1987, p. 133

14. Ibid.

15. Richard Cavendish, *The Black Arts*, G.P. Putnam's Sons, 1967, pp. 280, 281

16. Ibid.

17. Ibid.

18. Mike Warnke, *The Satan Seller*, Logos International, 1972, p. 101

CHAPTER 11 - OUT OF THE MOUTH OF THE DRAGON

1. *Spin*, September 1990, p. 58

2. *Spin*, February 1987, p. 46

3. *Musician* (Special Collectors Edition - Beatles and Rolling Stones), 1988, p. 20

4. *Star Parade*, Winter 1987, p. 6

5. *Rock & Soul*, August 1987, p. 6

6. *Rolling Stone*, October 18, 1990, p. 60

7. *BOP*, April 1990, p. 80

8. *Power Metal*, February 1988, p. 51

9. *Spin*, April 1989, p. 121

10. Dennis Corle, *The Pied Piper of Rock*, J.B. Printing Ministry, 1985, p. 13

11. Ibid., p. 98

12. *Spin*, September 1986, p.

13. Dan & Steve Peters, *Why Knock Rock*, Bethany House Publishers, 1984, p. 105

14. Fletcher A. Brothers, *The Rock Report*, Starburst Publishers, 1987, p. 51

15. Dennis Corle, *The Pied Piper of Rock*, J.B. Printing Ministry, 1985, p. 97

16. Ibid., p. 98

17. Bob Larson, *Rock*, Tyndale House Publishers Inc., 1984, p. 37

18. *Rock Yearbook Vol. 8*, St. Martins Press, 1988, p. 58

19. Dennis Corle, *The Pied Piper of Rock*, J.B. Printing Ministry, 1985, p. 88

20. Jeff Godwin, *Dancing with Demons*, Chick Publications, 1988, p. 47

21. Ibid., p. 94

22. Editors of Rolling Stone, *The Rolling Stone Interviews the 1980's*, St. Martins Press/Rolling Stone Press, 1989, p. 324

23. *Details*, October 1990, p. 86

24. Jeff Godwin, *Dancing with Demons*, Chick Publications, 1988, p. 155

25. *Rock Yearbook Vol. 8*, St. Martins Press, 1988, p. 70

CHAPTER 12 - WOODSTOCK: WE ARE THE WORLD/THE BEGINNING OF THE END

1. Jann S. Wenner (Ed.), *20 Years of Rolling Stones: What A Long Strange Trip It's Been*, Straight Arrow Publishers Inc., 1987, p. 50

2. Joel Makower, *Woodstock: The Oral History*, Doubleday Dell Publishing, 1989, p. 244

3. *Life*, August 1989, p. 23

CHAPTER 13 - NEW AGE MUSIC: CROSSING THE RAINBOW BRIDGE

1. *Reader's Digest*, October 1982, p. 203

2. *Meditation*, Winter 1990, p. 5

3. Ibid.

4. Ibid.

5. *Time*, January 2, 1989, pp. 29, 30

6. *Connecting Link*, 1989, Vol. 1, Issue 3, p. 31

7 Ibid.

CHAPTER 14 - FROM DARKNESS TO LIGHT

SELECTED BIBLIOGRAPHY

Aranza, Jacob. *Backwards Masking Unmasked.* Shreveport, La: Huntington House Inc., 1983.

Bramly, Serge. *Macumba: The Teachings of Maria-José, Mother of the Gods.* New York, N.Y.: Avon Books, 1977.

Brooke, Tal. *Riders of the Cosmic Circuit.* Batavia, Ill: Lion Publishing Company, 1986.

Brothers, Fletcher A. *The Rock Report.* Lancaster, Pa: Starburst Publishers, 1987.

Burdon, Eric. *I Used To Be An Animal, But I'm All Right Now.* Boston, Mass: Faber and Faber, 1986.

Cavendish, Richard. *The Black Arts.* New York, N.Y.: G.P. Putnam's Sons, 1967.

Corle, Dennis. *The Pied Piper of Rock.* J.B. Milford, Ohio: Printing Ministry, 1985.

Cranna, Ian, ed. *Rock Yearbook Vol. 8.* New York, N.Y.: St. Martins Press, 1988.

Crowley, Aleister. *Magick In Theory and Practice.* New York, N.Y.: Dover Publications, 1976.

-----------------. *The World's Tragedy.* Phoenix, Ariz.: Falcon Press, 1985.

Cumbey, Constance. *The Hidden Dangers of the Rainbow.* Shreveport, La: Huntington House, Inc., 1983.

Davis, Stephen. *Hammer of the Gods: The Led Zeppelin Story.* New York, N.Y.: Ballantine Books, 1985.

Davis, Wade. *The Serpent and the Rainbow.* New York, N.Y.: Warner Books, 1985.

Denning, Melita, and Osbourne Phillips. *Voudoun Fire: The Living Reality of Mystical Religion.* St. Paul, Minn.: Llewellyn Publications, 1979.

Edwards, Henry, and Tony Zanetta. *Stardust: The David Bowie Story.* New York, N.Y.: Bantam Books, 1987.

Eliade, Mircea. *Occultism Witchcraft and Cultural Fashions: Essays in Comparative Religions.* Chicago, Ill.: University of Chicago Press, 1976.

----------------. *Shamanism: Archaic Techniques of Ecstasy*. Princeton, N.J.: Princeton University Press, 1974.

----------------. *Yoga: Immortality and Freedom*. Princeton, N.J.: Princeton University Press, 1969.

Ferguson, Marilyn. *The Aquarian Conspiracy*. Los Angeles, Calif.: J.P. Tarcher, Inc., 1980.

Geller, Larry, and Joel Spector. *If I Can Dream: Elvis' Own Story*. New York, N.Y.: Simon & Shuster, 1989.

Godwin, Jeff. *Dancing with Demons*. Chino, Calif.: Chick Publications, 1988.

González-Wippler, Migene. *Santería: The Religion - A Legacy of Faith, Rites, and Magic*. New York, N.Y.: Harmony Books, 1989.

Graham, O.J. *The Six-Pointed Star*. Fletcher, N.C.: New Puritan Library, 1988.

Henderson, David. *'Scuse Me While I Kiss the Sky: The Life of Jimi Hendrix*. New York, N.Y.: Bantam Books, 1983.

Hopkins, Jerry, and Danny Sugerman. *No One Here Gets Out Alive*. New York, N.Y.: Warner Books, 1980.

Hounsome, Terry. *Rock Record*. New York, N.Y.: Facts on File Publications, 1987.

Hunt, Dave, and T.A. McMahon. *America: The Sorcerers New Apprentice*. Eugene, Ore.: Harvest House, 1988.

Ions, Veronica. *Indian Mythology*. London, England: Hamlyn Publishing, 1967

Kalweit, Holger. *Dreamtime & Inner Space: The World of the Shaman*. Boston, Mass.: Shambhala Publications, Inc., 1988.

King, Francis. *Sexuality, Magic and Perversion*. Secaucus, N.J.: The Citadel Press, 1972.

Larson, Bob. *Rock*. Wheaton, Ill.: Tyndale House Publishers Inc., 1984.

LaVey, Anton Szandor. The Satanic Bible. New York, N.Y.: Avon Books, 1969.

Lewis, I.M. *Ecstatic Religion: A Study of Shamanism and Spirit Possession*. New York, N.Y.: Routledge, 1989.

Maharaj, Rabi. *Death of a Guru*. Eugene, Ore.: Harvest House Publishers, 1984.

Makower, Joel. *Woodstock: The Oral History*. New York, N.Y.: Doubleday Dell Publishing, 1989.

Maple, Eric. *Witchcraft*. London, England: Octopus Books, 1973.

Metraux, Alfred. *Voodoo in Haiti*. New York, N.Y.: Shocken Books, 1972.

Miller, Jim, ed. *The Rolling Stone Illustrated History of Rock & Roll*. New York, N.Y.: Rolling Stone Press, 1980.

Peters, Dan & Steve. *Why Knock Rock*. Minneapolis, Minn.: Bethany House Publishers, 1984.

Raleigh, Dr. A.S. *Occult Geometry*. Marina del Rey, Calif.: DeVorss & Co., 1981.

Robertson, Sandy. *The Aleister Crowley Scrapbook*. York Beach, Maine: Samuel Weiser Inc., 1988.

Rolling Stone, eds. *The Rolling Stone Interviews the 1980's*. New York, N.Y.: St. Martins Press/Rolling Stone Press, 1989.

Rouget, Gilbert. *Music and Trance: A Theory of the Relations Between Music and Possession*. Chicago, Ill.: The University of Chicago Press, 1985.

St. Clair, David. *Say You Love Satan*. New York, N.Y.: Dell Publishing, 1987.

Sanchez, Tony. *Up and Down with The Rolling Stones*. New York, N.Y.: Signet Books, 1979.

Shapiro, Harry. *Waiting for the Man: The Story of Drugs and Popular Music*. Great Britain: Quartet Books Ltd., 1988.

Schwartz, Ted, and Duane Empey. *Satanism: Is Your Family Safe*. Grand Rapids, Mich.: Zondervan Publishing House, 1988.

Spitz, Robert Steven. *Barefoot in Babylon*. New York, N.Y.: Norton, 1989.

Steiger, Brad. *Demon Lovers*. New Brunswick, N.J.: Inner Light Publications, 1896.

Sugerman, Danny. *The Doors Illustrated History*. New York, N.Y.: William Morrow and Company, 1983.

Symonds, John, and Kenneth Grant, eds. *The Confessions of Aleister Crowley*. New York, N.Y.: Bantam Books, 1971.

Taylor, Derek. *It Was Twenty Years Ago Today: An Anniversary Celebration of 1967*. New York, N.Y.: Simon & Shuster, 1987.

Tosches, Nick. Hellfire: *The Jerry Lee Lewis Story*. New York, N.Y.: Bantam/Doubleday/Dell Publishing Group, 1982.

Ward, Ed, and Geoffrey Stokes, and Ken Tucker. *Rock of Ages: The History of Rock & Roll*. Englewood Cliffs, N.J.: Rolling Stone Press, 1986.

Warnke, Mike. *The Satan Seller*. Plainfield, N.J.: Logos International, 1972.

Wenner, Jann S., ed. 20 Years of Rolling Stones: What A Long Strange Trip It's Been. New York, N.Y.: Straight Arrow Publishers Inc., 1987.

White, Charles. The Life and Times of Little Richard. New York, N.Y.: Harmony Books, 1984.

White, Timothy. Rock Lives. New York, N.Y.: Henry Holt and Co., Inc., 1990.

Wilson, Colin. Aleister Crowley: The Nature of The Beast. Northamptonshire, England: Aquarian Press, 1987.

Yogananda, Paramahansa. Autobiography of a Yogi. 10th printing. Los Angeles, Calif.: Self-Realization Fellowship, 1988.

York, Ritchie. The Led Zeppelin Biography. New York, N.Y.: Methuen Publications, 1976.

INDEX

242

Colombia, 131

Columbia Records, 39, 40

Communism, 71

Confessions of Aleister Crowley, The, 81

Continental Drift (song), 98

Connecting Link (magazine), 219

Cooke, Sam, 27

Cooper, Alice, 17, 157

Cope, Julian, 154

Country Joe & The Fish (band), 78

Coven (band), 165-168

Coverdale, David, 154

Cream, The, (band), 60, 63, 78

Crosby, David, 78, 189

Crosby, Stills, Nash, and Young, (band), 78, 189

Cross (of Christ), 64, 65, 94, 126, 141, 157, 164, 212, 226, 230

Crowley, Aleister, 60, 61, 81-87, 90-94, 97-99, 101, 129, 137, 138

 - anti-Christ attitude of, 72, 83

 - Christian background, 82, 83

 - Great Beast, The, (*aka* Master Therion), 81-85

 - Hinduism and, 72, 90

 - law ("Do What Thou Wilt"), 86, 87, 90, 101

crucifix, 64, 65, 158, 159, 221

crystal power (*see also* occult practices), 210

Cult, The, (band), 17

Cumbey, Constance, 197, 217

Cummings, Burton, 17

Cure, The, (band), 158

Cygnus X-1 Book 1 - The Voyage, (song), 133

D

Daltrey, Roger, v, 89

dancing

 - trance inducing/ceremonial, 9-12, 18, 37, 38, 49, 54, 99, 148, 183, 200

 - sex and, 12-17

Danzig (band), 86, 120-127

 - "Home Video", 122, 125

Danzig, Glenn, 86, 101, 122-127

Danzig II-LUCIFUGE (album), 126

Dark Horse (album), 206

darkness, forces/powers of, 19, 20, 31, 46, 106, 107, 113, 120, 125, 139, 142, 185, 229 (*see also* demons/devils)

Davis, Stephen, 95

Davis, Wade, 36-38

Dawn of Megiddo (song), 141

Days of Future Passed (album), 203

Day the Earth Stood Still, The, (movie), 130

Dead Kennedys (band), 161

Dear God (song - Midge Ure), 213

Dear God (song - XTC), 162

death

 - entry of into the world, 46

 - Hindu affinity towards, 45, 59, 203, 209

 - imagery of in Rock & Roll, 44, 58, 59, 115, 141, 167

 - of Jesus/Jesus' resurrection from, 65, 94, 95, 155, 178, 226

 - of Lucifer/Satan, 3, 4, 186

 - Kali, goddess of, 75-77, 103-105

 - magnitude of in the Great Tribulation, 5, 223, 224

 - mockery of Jesus', 64, 69, 126, 141, 147, 156, 159, 164, 165, 166

 - obituaries

   Stiv Bators, 101

   Marc Bolan, 99

   Graham Bond, 61, 101

   John Bonham, 97

   Aleister Crowley, 86

   Aleister Crowley's father, 83

   Sandy Denny, 95, 97

   Esquerita, 30

   Jimi Hendrix, 52, 155, 156

   Brian Jones, 98

H

J

O

T

W

"World Teacher", 193

X

XTC (band), 153, 162

Y

Yale University, 54
Yantras (*see also* Hinduism), 103-105, 201-204
Yardbirds, The, (band), 63, 89
Yasgur, Max, 179
Yaweh, 163
Yes (band), 195-198
Yin Yang, 206
Yoga, 12, 75, 111, 112, 182, 183, 188, 198, 203, 216, 222
Yoga: Immortality and Freedom, 12
Yogananda, Paramahansa, 71, 190, 196
yogi(c)(s), 9, 12, 44-46, 50, 59, 71, 74, 75, 77, 129, 182, 183, 190, 196, 198, 203, 220, 226
Yoruba (*see also* Voodoo), 35, 54
Young, Neil, 78, 187
You're All I Need (song), 116

Z

Zodiaque (album), 199

HEARTBEAT OF THE DRAGON ORDER FORM

NAME _____

ADDRESS _____

CITY _____

STATE _____ ZIP _____

COUNTRY _____

PHONE # (_____) _____

We also have a monthly newsletter available dealing with the latest developments in the subject areas of Rock & Roll/New Age Music; Satanism/Occultism; and the New Age Movement/New World Order. To order the newsletter, "The Light Warrior", send check or money order in U.S. funds payable to:

Light Warrior Press, Ltd.
P.O. Box 7017
Sterling Heights, MI 48311.

QTY	DESCRIPTION	PRICE@	COST
	The Heartbeat of the Dragon	$11.95	
	The Light Warrior Newsletter	**	
		TAX*	
		S&H	
		TOTAL	

*Michigan residents add 4% sales tax

**The Light Warrior *Subscription rates:*

3rd Class - $30.00/1 yr.   1st Class - $36.00/1 yr.   Foreign ------- $48.00/1 yr.
$52.00/2 yrs. $64.00/2 yrs.   (Incl. Canada) $88.00/2 yrs.

Shipping & Handling for each book - $1.75
(please allow 6-8 weeks delivery for books)

*Mark Spaulding is also available for speaking engagements. For booking info contact:
The Christian Militia at 1-(313)-247-8186 or write to:*

The Christian Militia
P.O. Box 7017
Sterling Heights, MI 48311